FLYING FLEA
HENRI MIGNET'S POU-DU-CIEL

Arthur W. J. G. Ord-Hume

Henri Mignet was born on October 19th, 1893, at Charente-Maritime. At an early age he demonstrated his inventive ability, making wireless receivers (radio sets). He also trained as a furniture-maker. His long life was not without tragedy and more than a fair share of failure but when he died on August 31st 1965 at Ain Harronda, Morocco, the whole world of amateur aviation mourned the passing of a man who had carved himself a justly-earned niche in aviation history. Taken from the French magazine *Les Cahiers due RSA* (the journal of the Roseau due Sport de lair) for January 1967 is this fine image of Henri Mignet seated in one of his later machines. Not without just cause can he be described as the man who began the entire homebuilt aircraft movement across the world.

Opposite: In 1946, Henri Mignet advertised his new version of the Flying Flea – the HM-290 Le Sport de l'Air. It was promoted by the short-lived aviation magazine *L'Aéronef* edited in Brussels by Odilon Dubois. This is the multi-coloured artwork on the folder that contained the one drawing which made up the 'set of plans', presented on a single sheet of paper 42 1/2-inches wide by 28 inches deep. Every part was filled with Henri Mignet's detailed drawings and neatly hand-written instructions – in French. For the benefit of foreigners, there was a separate long sheet of newsprint printed double-sided with translations into English, Dutch, French (presumably for reference), Italian and German.

Henri Mignet conducted many experiments with primitive gliders. During 1923 he flew five versions of his hang-glider design, most, such as this one, having no vertical tail surface. Trials at Vauville involved half a dozen helpers (usually young women) tugging on a tow rope while the budding aviator ran along, his glider thoughtfully provided with a tailwheel. This, the HM-5, was his most successful but finally he had to admit it flew best with a large rudder.

Further Reading

Ellis, Ken, and Jones, Geoffrey P: *Henri Mignet and his Flying Fleas*. Haynes, Sparkford, 1990

Le Pou du Ciel, French language newsletter, Michel Jacquet, Amicale Pouducieliste, 30 rue Bourdon de St Amans, 47240 Bob-Encontre, France

Mignet, Henri: *The Flying Flea (Le Pou-du-Ciel): How to Build and Fly It*. Translated from the French by The Air League of the British Empire, London, 1936. (several impressions & reprints)

Ord-Hume, Arthur W J G: *The First Home-built Aeroplanes*. Stenlake, Catrine, 2009. [contains reprints of all the *Practical Mechanics* Flying Flea construction articles]

Ord-Hume, Arthur W J G: *British Light Aeroplanes*. GMS Enterprises, Peterborough, 2000

Pou Renew, Newsletter of the English language Flying Flea group. HMS, PO Box 101194, Chicago, Illinois 60610, USA.

Acknowledgements

For permission to use photographs: *Flight International, The Aeroplane, Popular Flying* (1935), Richard Riding, George Cull, Mike Hooks, Bob Littlejohn, the late Harold Best-Devereux, the late Don Burgoyne. Picture quality is variable and some illustrations are presented on grounds of rarity rather than perfection. Some were taken by an enthusiastic child with a Box Brownie: my photography has, happily, improved with age: the old photos, however, cannot.

© 2011 Arthur W. J. G. Ord-Hume
First Published in the United Kingdom, 2011
Stenlake Publishing Limited
54-58 Mill Square, Catrine, KA5 6RD
01290 551122
www.stenlake.co.uk

ISBN 9781840335545

Cover Illustration: This is taken from the cover of *Popular Flying* for November 1935 and the artwork is by the famous artist Howard Leigh (1896-1981) who at that time provided some illustrations for W E Johns' magazine.

INTRODUCTION

It is now more than three-quarters of a century since a benevolent-looking Frenchman, complete with beret, proclaimed to the world that anybody – *everybody*, in fact – could make one of his tiny wooden aeroplanes on the kitchen table. And it was cheaper to build than the cost of a family car!

Would-be amateur flyers around the globe grasped the offer with eager hands. A bit like that character in BBC Radio's famous *Goon Show* programme, Bluebottle, they all chanted 'Yes! I *can* build an aeroplane!' Many did, but, as events panned out, it mostly ended in tears…

These were flying's pre-supersonic days, long before the jet engine at a time when all aeroplanes had propellers. Airspace (meaning the sky) was neither restricted nor carved into invisible highways that demanded radio communication. Unless you were seriously competitive and wanted to fly your lightplane to India or Australia, private flying was simple, uncomplicated and not terribly 'high-tech'.

As for the aeroplanes themselves, they were simple. Their pilots needed only to have obtained an 'A' Licence which was not too difficult to get and demanded neither impossible financial investment nor extensive knowledge and practice. Many aircraft, even flying club machines, had only rudimentary instrumentation. The majority didn't even carry a compass. In those times, navigation was by eyeball which meant a mixture of map-reading and looking over the cockpit side. It was known as 'Bradshawing' your way around the country named after the famous guide to railway services set up in 1841 by George Bradshaw (1801-1853).

Mind you, aircraft flew both low and slow so fixing your position from a road, railway line or church steeple was easier than setting a compass course and mathematically correcting for a crosswind which tended to blow you in another direction. Poor visibility (fog and an almost perpetual industrial haze were ever-present problems in the 1930s and persisted right up to the 1950s) and long-distance flights did, of course, suggest the precaution of taking the magnetic needle on board but, for general flying, seeing your way was the private pilot's way of finding his destination.

Flying and aeroplanes were exciting! The era of the air-display and five-shilling joy-ride (usually in an old and terminally senile Avro 504K fitted with an elderly oil-spraying rotary engine that incongruously whizzed round in company with the propeller) was at its height. Sir Alan Cobham, that great promoter of aviation for the masses, took his National Aviation Day displays – popularly known as Cobham's Flying Circus – all over the country. His was not the only travelling air show: there were plenty of others including C W A Scott, Cornwall Aviation Co, Surrey Flying Services and so on.

But *owning* an aeroplane was beyond both dreams and the pockets of most people. Everybody knew that! The £100 motor car was barely affordable so the average man could never be expected to lay out the £350 needed for a brand new Moth, not even £200 for a second-hand Avro Avian. Unless you were very wealthy, that is. And that sort of wealth was scarce as Britain struggled to overcome the 1930s recession. The average wage for most was no more than £200 a year with many surviving on just thirty shillings a week.

Building your own aircraft posed a possible way out of this situation. There was, however, a stumbling-block in making anything flyable at home – and it was a pretty big one. Quite simply, you were not *allowed* to! Restrictions and regulations had been systematically introduced in Britain since the end of the 1914-18 war which closed up and removed any last vestige of 'window of opportunity'. You might *build* an aeroplane, but you could not register it and without a registration you could not insure it and without registration or insurance you couldn't fly it – legally at any rate!

The editor of the weekly magazine *The Aeroplane*, Charles G Grey, published a story in the issue of February 18th, 1933, where, on page 277 and under the headline 'Home-Made Aeroplanes', he wrote: 'Present British regulations make the building of home-made aeroplanes practically impossible.' Our restrictions were far stricter than those in America where, in 1932, some 225 identification numbers (the US equivalent of our registration letters) were issued for home-made aircraft. Only about a third of these would reach the flying stage and of these, half would be the familiar designs of Heath, Pietenpol and Church – all types for which plans or kits of parts were available. To power these, aircraft engines were seldom employed and around half the home-made machines used modified motor-cycle engines while the remainder mainly used converted Ford car engines.

HM-14 G-ADSD was the fourth example to by built by Mignet in Paris and was fitted with a 25 hp Poinsard motor. Bought by N A D Displays Ltd of Ford on September 11th 1935, it was sold that December to W G Bennett of Aldenham. It crashed the following March.

It was a sad state of affairs in the UK. Aviation was barely 30 years old and already officialdom had stepped in to ensure that the ordinary man should not be allowed to meddle with it! This conveniently overlooked the fact that the aviation pioneers were, by definition, amateurs!

A generation of frustrated ex-wartime flyers were limited to flying club and private-owner aircraft and those who had ideas for their own personal aerial runabouts were left in fear of the dire consequences of contravening the Laws of the Land.

And so, when this Frenchman came along and offered us the chance to build one of his curious *Pou-du-Ciel* aeroplanes for £25, well, the response was predictable. OK, by the time you had bought a decent engine for it the cost probably soared to nearer £65, but that was still just about affordable, especially if three or four of you got together and formed a construction club to pool labour and finances. Being English and all that, we quickly anglicized the name to *The Flying Flea*.

It was the birth of an era unique in the aviation world. Not only did it germinate the latent seed for flying that lay so long dormant in the breasts of many, but it forced the authorities to find a way of letting these things fly legally. And the man who fought Authority and won was Henri Mignet.

Now you might justifiably think that the world would celebrate the man for such an achievement. Not a bit of it for we find that history has been more than a little unkind to one of light aviation's greatest inventors and his achievements. Not until after he had departed for that clubhouse in the sky would Mignet attain his just reward.

Back, then, to the 1930s – a time when flying still had that rich, almost primordial fascination for many people, mostly (but not exclusively) male, largely young but all deeply enthusiastic for things that flew and the people who flew them. The sky offered adventure and excitement!

Which is why Henri Mignet, who had started out as an amateur radio dabbler in his native part of France – Charente-Maritime – suddenly became the talk of not just Europe but of the whole world. His funny little aeroplane ended up being built in almost every part of the globe from Finland to New Zealand, Canada to Australia, and (in Britain) from St Just to Thurso.

Today's home-built aeroplane movement owes much to the genius of Henri Mignet and his *Pou-du-Ciel*. It was he who single-handedly demystified the mystique that had been built around aviation, aeronautics and, above all, aeroplane construction after the First World War, It was he who pointed out that having been started by amateurs, despite being usurped by military needs, it was high time flying was returned to the hands of amateurs.

The modern home-made aircraft is very different from those of Mignet's era. Materials, including high-tech synthetics that were unheard of in the 1930s, combine with large and lightweight engines to offer construction procedures completely foreign to the wood-and-fabric of his era, while the 21st century homebuilt possesses flight characteristics and a performance that our forefathers might only ever have dreamed of.

Present-day amateur flyers are technophobes by necessity! And home-built aircraft have flown around the world and across the vast oceans without problem. In so doing they have broken many long-established records. As for instrumentation, modern navigation and communication equipment plus GPS devices virtually dispense with any need for maps, while friendly round-dial instruments with moving needles have been replaced by the 'glass' instrument panel that provides a lot of detailed flight information on coloured computer screens. Flyers today fly in perpetual dread of a 'System error: Closing down' message…

The question is whether Henri Mignet would even identify the modern homebuilt as being the work of the amateur constructor! For a long time it has been understood that there is a vast gulf of a difference between the words 'amateurish' and 'amateur'. The former is the work of the unaccomplished and over-exuberant unskilled artisan: the latter is the work of somebody who may be professional in his standard of work yet does it for nothing but the love of the achievement. It is this rich difference between two similar-sounding words that get confused in the minds of some people. I have seen many an amateur-built aircraft finished to a far higher standard than a factory-produced machine.

Some of the plastic 'kit-planes' that are put together from pre-manufactured and pre-assembled parts can also rival in finish and appearance the best of the production aeroplanes. Mignet might just have understood that all this was the inevitable outcome of three-quarters of a century of improvement. He would, however, be horrified at the technical and aerodynamic work that lies behind the amateur aircraft of the 21st century. The mathematics, the testing and the paperwork needed is of daunting proportions. Mignet, with the best will in the world, was a simple and uncomplicated man who drove everywhere on an aged motorcycle and who so commendably eliminated everything that was unnecessary in his aircraft to save money, effort and time. Paperwork, in his scheme, was quite redundant!

The only problem was that Mignet was 100 percent self-taught in that empirical college where success is achieved through trial and error accompanied by bruises and bandages rather than through the application of science and mathematics. He had the good fortune to find success but it was garnered at high cost. The highly-educated aeronautists looked down their noses at his efforts and were the first to shout 'Told you so!' when the endeavour began to go pear-shaped. But here's the incontrovertible fact of history! Nobody really remembers those clever engineers who saw where they thought Mignet was wrong – but everybody remembers Henri Mignet! Is it because he was the joker in the pack – a sort of Florence Foster Jenkins of the aircraft world? Or can it be that he was as influential as a few savants suspected at the time?

Well, this is supposed to be a brief illustrated account of Henri Mignet and his little aeroplane. First, though, I must come clean and admit to bias! Yes, I was a convert to the Flying Flea. And, yes, I did start to build one. But to begin with we have to go back those 75 and more long years to tell you how and why…

Prelude and Infection

I was an extremely small schoolboy, spotty of complexion and possessed of a full complement of those characteristics that make extremely small schoolboys so obnoxious. I had condescended to hold my mother's hand – in itself something extremely small schoolboys only do under duress – so that she should not get lost in the disparate throng of people standing around the edge of a small and windy field by the waterfront at Bournemouth.

The purpose of this seemingly pointless exercise was apparently to welcome a Frenchman from the skies who, said the *Daily Express* placards and loudspeakers around the field, was expected imminently. I did not know what 'imminently' meant but concluded that it was something to do with having a long wait and being bored. Yes, sure, I was interested in aeroplanes, but only (I thought) in those really big fast silver biplane fighters that the Royal Air Force flew at Hendon. Or the ones they tied together with coloured ribbon and did formation aerobatics in. How was I to know that the ribbon was really elastic cord so it wouldn't break!

I enjoyed those sleek biplanes as they roared upwards, paused and then turned over in a loop with bracing wires singing, superchargers screaming and fabric thrumming. The noise was thrilling and the whine when the aircraft flew past very low was exciting.

I also liked the huge Spartan three-seater biplane that gave joy-rides from the little Apse Heath aerodrome off Landguard Manor Road at Shanklin on the Isle of Wight where we usually spent our summer holidays. This year, though, we had had to come to Bournemouth where my father had some coincidental business to sort out. And that was why I had to stand in a field holding Mummy's hand and feeling a bit of a lemon.

But standing in a field waiting for a flying Frenchman was not quite the same thing as watching the flying at Hendon. For a start everybody knew that it wasn't a big silver biplane with a roaring Rolls-Royce motor, but a home-made plane with the engine off a motor-bike. I had a home-made plane. It was a Frog self-assembly kit, it lived in a box and was powered by knicker elastic, not that I really knew what knicker-elastic was in those days – except that it was rubber and rude.

The sun wasn't exactly beating down on the grass that day. In fact it was cloudy, rather cold and more than a bit breezy. Which made the whole business a bit more tolerable because the seashore was probably a bit too cold for paddling, sand-castles and kicking the beach into innocent peoples' faces.

And then we heard it. In an instant all heads turned, faces aligned with raised arms terminating in extended forefingers pointing at the horizon, and people shouted 'Look!' An incredibly small melange of wings and other bits had suddenly appeared very close and seemingly travelling very fast and low down. And then the engine stopped and without so much as a fly-around it was down in the grass, a truly tiny insect-like plane banging and bouncing along with a stationary propeller. It sounded like somebody kicking a large drum down a flight of stairs as tautly-doped fabric thrummed and tiny wheelbarrow wheels traversed the bumpy sod. People applauded.

I was looking at my first-ever Flying Flea!

The Epidemic

Back in those inter-war years with their troubled politics and threatening skies, Britain was experiencing the peak of the *Flying Flea* craze as would-be amateur flyers eagerly glued and nailed plywood and spruce to try to copy the achievements of the Frenchman. It was in 1935 that Henri Mignet emulated Louis Blèriot and crossed *la Manche* in his diminutive wooden aeroplane which he had built himself not in a great workshop, but in his miniscule apartment. His achievement rocked the world of amateur aviation and set up shock waves that still permeate the world of home-builders and would-be flyers to this day. If the Wright Brothers take credit for starting this flying business, then it was Mignet who brought flying to the man in the street.

Quickly sponsored by one of Britain's aeronautically-aware popular newspapers, the aircraft and its designer embarked on a demonstration tour of the British Isles.

Not since 1909 when Blériot arrived in his Monoplane had an invasion received such a public acclaim! Everybody wanted to own one of these little aeroplanes and when the affable designer produced a book telling just how to make it, the result exceeded anybody's wildest dreams. By 1936, Fleas were being built across the nation. Stories about this extraordinary little aeroplane appeared in all the press and even the satirical magazine *Punch* published a large cartoon featuring one of the aircraft at a stately home.

The original *Flying Flea* with its tandem wings, no proper tail and, usually, a motorcycle-type engine screaming away at the front end has long-since departed our skies, yet the enthusiasm for home-built aircraft that it sired is still with us today. The irony is that the passing years have proved that the emotions and ideas generated by this derided French-designed curiosity were the seeds from which so much of amateur aviation the world over have grown.

A good deal has been written about the *Flying Flea* over the years. A bit like the proverbial 'bad penny', the thing does not go away, for the all-too brief era of this tiny aeroplane is widely remembered for all the wrong reasons. Generations have been brought up to ridicule it. Countless people recall its name for second-hand reasons that, in the majority of cases, are actually quite wrong. Somebody, who was obviously biased, included it in a book devoted to 'the world's worst aircraft' – although the author failed to define what he meant by 'worst'.

Henri Mignet on the propeller of his HM-16 with its 32 hp Moteur Mengin flat twin-cylinder engine. The pilot is either a late arrival or has suddenly remembered pressing business elsewhere.

People quote its designer as saying 'if you can knock together a packing-case then you can build my aeroplane!' This was a mistake and he should never have said it, for it diminished his credibility in a flash. Years later one Gerald Ratner would commit commercial suicide with the same sort of ill-chosen, off-the-cuff comment. Mignet also encouraged people to teach themselves to fly in his aeroplane. That, too, was an unwise piece of advice which he probably lived to regret.

And so people think they remember the Flying Flea as the one plane that was so notorious that it was probibited. Almost everybody who writes about the Flea ends up saying it was banned. Not true! It was never 'banned' as such.

But most of all, people remember that it killed 'a lot of people' in Britain: some think dozens or even more. Again, not true!

I have revealed more than a passing interest in Flying Fleas for, as a young lad and after that windy day at Bournemouth, I met the designer and watched his flying demonstration. It was a moment of truth for I rushed home and started to build one! A bit like malaria, once you have been infected with amateur aircraft construction, it returns at regular intervals to haunt you! And I had just been bitten by a *Flea*…

Potted History of the Pou

At the age of eleven, Henri Mignet entered the Lycée de Nantes but from early on he was thinking about flight. By the time he was eighteen he was in correspondence with Gustav Lilienthal (1849-1933), younger brother of the German glider pioneer Otto (1848-1896). This got him interested in the possibilities of gliding and at least two rather basic machines were built. Real success eluded these experiments.

When it came to trying to fly a conventional aeroplane, Mignet was, by his own admission, something of a clummock who could not co-ordinate hands and feet to manipulate ailerons, elevators and rudder. There were, he reckoned, simply too many controls to remember! While countless other mortals managed the complexities of the world's Avros, Moths and Bluebirds, Mignet decided to do away with as many of these formal controls as he could and produce a simple plane that he could fly. And that meant *anybody* could fly!

His experiments began in earnest as early as 1923 and in that year one of his prototype aircraft, a curious if mostly-conventional parasol monoplane having huge ailerons, lifting tailplane and no rudder, appeared at Orly for tests. Illustrated in *Flight* for June 14th, this was the HM-4: its ultimate fate is not recorded but it was to be the precursor of a series of lightplane designs. The failure of his earlier machines was, however, too public for the designer who immediately decided that all his further experiments would be carried out far from the eyes of spectators.

He persevered and designed and built in his Paris suburban apartment a succession of small aeroplanes, each building on the experience gained from its predecessor. His only transport was an old motorbike and sidecar but using this he towed his creations to a secluded piece of land some 200 km NE of Paris where he lived. It was called the Plain of Beaurepaire close to the villages of Vailly, Chassemy and Comdé.

Here he set up a camp-site on a piece of land surrounded by birch woods and carried on experimenting for more than a decade. By the early 1930s he was making aircraft to what he called his formula which now centred on controlling a rudder not with the feet as usual, but with the control-column, moving it to the side to turn in a chosen direction. And pulling back on the 'stick' did not work an elevator, but increased the incidence of the front wing.

In 1933, Mignet had completed his trials and come up with his fourteenth and most successful machine, suitably designated the HM-14. It took exactly one month to build. He named it *Le Sport de l'Air* and, on September 10th, 1933, made the first 'aerial hop' from his campsite. Three weeks later, on November 8th, 1933, he completed the first circuit. He quickly built up ten flying hours whereupon he decided he would write a book extolling its virtues. The book, like the aircraft, was called *Le Sport de l'Air* and prefaced a first showing before an astonished crowd at the 1934 Salon de l'Aéronautique exhibition in Paris. The proper public debut happened at Orly on December 9th. He now went so far as to proclaim, famously, that his aeroplane was so safe that you could teach yourself to fly it in a weekend! By now the name *Pou-de-Ciel* (literally 'louse of the sky') had been coined – and stuck.

The magazine *Les Ailes* was captivated and its editor, Georges Houard (who had long advocated cheaper and more popular flying) championed the cause of Mignet and his *Poux*. The French, not generally associated with popular uprisings, uprose in their masses. Mignet's book, in which, to the accompaniment of much colourful Gallic rhetoric, he showed the reader how to build his own *Pou-du-Ciel*, became an overnight best-seller, reprints being called for up to 1937.

But however top-selling it was, his book displayed a glaring shortcoming. Mignet was happy to tell us of his successes but never of his trials. We search in vain for details of his countless experiments, design changes and improvements, his results and, just as important, his failures. And we quickly find that not only was he an inexperienced flyer but equally he was no test pilot. Not for him the careful probing of a flight performance envelope and the creation of parameters. Centres of gravity and pressure, centroids, fundamental aerodynamics – all were evidently beyond his ken. He made an aeroplane that worked by trial and error and that, to him, was all that mattered.

The Flying Flea was quite different from anything else ever seen in our skies. Its designer was an entirely self-taught designer-builder who schemed out his little *Pou-du-Ciel* (which translates as 'Skylouse', hence the common English *Flying Flea*) to incorporate his own individual control system. He considered it more intuitive than the scheme fostered by his countryman Louis Blèriot with his famous *cloche*. Instead, Mignet used only a control stick which, when moved left to right, moved the rudder, and when moved forward and back pivoted the entire main wing about its front spar. There were no ailerons and no elevators and the pilot's feet were not required to do anything clever at all!

Fleas Colonise Britain

Flea mania had already swept through France and its arrival in Britain caused concern in high places. However, home-building had never been seen by the Air Ministry (which at that time was responsible for all flying including civil aircraft) as a threat to sanity or national security. Accordingly it was totally unprepared for the 'Flea tsunami' that followed. And the men in Whitehall had no notion as to what they were letting themselves in for.

The highly-respected Air League of the British Empire championed Mignet and his crusade to encourage the ordinary man in the street to build his own aeroplane. An English translation of the book by Mignet was arranged. Called *The Flying Flea*, it was prefaced by a glowing introduction penned by Air Commodore John Adrian Chamier, CB, CMG, DSO, OBE (1883-1974). Chamier was an immensely influential man. Although by that time retired, this decorated First World War pilot remained a highly-respected figure in aviation. He went on to establish the Air Training Corps but in the meanwhile his endorsement of Mignet's Flea was all that was needed to convince even the sceptics that home-made aeroplanes were suddenly the flavour of the month.

The book was a triumph! In dispensing with a good deal of the florid French hyperbole, the English version was, consequently, much shorter than the original. Nevertheless the first edition of 6,000 copies appeared in 1935 and sold out in less than a month! A reprint was hastily organised – and the title continued to sell to a public captivated by the thought of building and flying their own aircraft. Ownership of a copy seemed to be the fashion statement of the age!

Mignet's book was certainly inspirational. It is also highly dangerous to read today for the enthusiasm is so infectious that even sane men have been known to contemplate building one after opening its pages.

Pride before the Fall

Stephen Villers Appleby was a young Englishman who had spent some time in France. Here he met up with Mignet and actually built and flew one of his earlier machines. Now back home, he lost no time in building what would be among the first British-built Fleas.

Under pressure from Chamier's Air League, the Air Ministry grudgingly agreed to issue the Flea with an 'Authorisation to Fly', a special type of poor man's Certificate of Airworthiness that was created for home-built aeroplanes.

And so the first British Flea to fly – and crash – was that of 23-year-old Stephen Appleby at the one-time Heston Airport to the west of London and today within the limits of Heathrow. Now Mignet had devised his aircraft to be built in a small room rather than a large workshop. Consequently he made it as tiny as possible. He tried flying on wings that spanned just four metres – about thirteen feet – but found that five

G-ADPW was built by E G Perman Ltd for R G Doig of Lympne and gained its authorisation to fly on October 18th 1935. It later performed with Campbell Black's Circus. It survived until 1939. Here Doig poses with his machine while his wife occupies the cockpit. Jean Batten's famous Percival Gull is just visible, right.

After the 1939-45 War, Henri Mignet produced his first peace-time Flea as a tribute to his wife, Annette, who had been killed in the conflict. Here is a terrible snapshot of the memorable moment when the HM-290 made its maiden flight.

metres or 16$\frac{1}{4}$ feet was better. However, he went on to recommend no less than six metres (19$\frac{1}{2}$ feet) if you wanted to carry enough fuel for several hours' flying, if you weighed more than 60 kilos – or if you had a heavy engine.

Appleby was not overweight – but his engine most definitely was. His aircraft used a perfectly ordinary Ford 10 water-cooled motor-car engine. This made for a very heavy installation. Add to this a large car radiator and everything else, it also created a good deal of aerodynamic drag. All this combined to render Appleby's selection of a five-metre span rather on the optimistic side.

On Sunday afternoon, July 14th 1935, Appleby decided to try out his handiwork which had been checked over by the engineers at Airwork. It was a cool day with a favourable wind. The Flea flew although it was apparent to those watching that it was rather underpowered.

The *Daily Express,* arguably the nation's most aviation-minded broadsheet newspaper, decided to sponsor a nationwide tour of Appleby and his aircraft just as it had done with Mignet when first the Frenchman had introduced his little machine to British skies. To launch the event a gala photo-call was arranged for the morning of Monday, July 29th. Appleby posed with his handiwork and was pictured beneath one of Jersey Airways' huge four-engined de Havilland airliners (G-ACZP). This is shown on page 20.

With most of the nation's press in attendance, Appleby started up the Ford motor and prepared for his flight into history. Unlike two Sundays earlier, it was a roaster of a day and the mini-heat wave that had arrived in Britain that weekend took temperatures well into the high seventies Fahrenheit. Moreover, there was no wind and the windsock dangled listlessly.

Enter the Movie Mogul

At this point in the story it is necessary to digress a moment and introduce a peripheral character from outside the aviation world who actually played a part in that very public and unfortunate demonstration on that far-off summer's day.

The greatest movie mogul of the 1930s and 1940s was Hungarian-born Alexander Korda (1893-1956). He is best remembered for films like *Things to Come* and *The Third Man.* Korda was a dedicated anglophile, and soon created the famous Denham Film Studios and his trademark 'London Films' with its Big Ben logo.

In 1935, he had the idea of making a film called *The Conquest of the Air* to tell the story of flight. He got the firm of E D Abbott of Farnham, coachmakers and glider-builders, to create an assortment of historic reconstructions for the film and, without much of a script, began shooting.

Despite starring Laurence Olivier, it was a truly dreadful film! It lacked a plan, proper direction and even a sense of purpose. Five years in the making – it was not released until 1940 – to a well-deserved critics' panning. But it has proved to be an historic work because, soon after work began on it, Korda was included in the invitations to the Heston bean-feast to witness Appleby preparing for his 'first' Flea flight. Unaccountably switching direction from historic documentary to newsreel mode, Korda actually filmed Appleby's fateful flight – and subsequent crash – and left it in as part of his film.

True the actual prang is modestly just out of shot and all one sees is the cloud of dust as the *Flea* hits dry ground, but it does much to explain *why* he crashed. Watching his flight one can see that he was never really in controlled flight, the machine being underpowered for his wing-area and all-up weight. And it did not 'land upside down' but came to ground in level flight, only turning over after it had hit a ploughed field.

What happened was that the high-revving direct-drive Ford motor with its fine-pitch propeller struggled to find useful air to work in. The *Flea* rumbled along Heston's grass surface making tentative brief hops before Appleby managed to make one hop 'stick' – and stay in the air. But he had no climbing speed and certainly insufficient height in which to turn. He later said that, realising he had insufficient urge to stay flying, he decided to land straight ahead. By now he was outside the airfield boundary and skimming a field of rough dry ploughed earth. He hit a clod of earth and promptly inverted, smashing the sharply-curved main wing with the weight of the aircraft, and collapsing the big rudder.

The press had their picture, but hopes of a demonstration flight, let alone the 'round-Britain' tour were dashed. The same week as Appleby's inversion at Heston, Air Cmdr Chamier's own Flea turned upside down at Heston. It was a taste of what was to come.

The Coach-builder and the Car Engine

Former RFC pilot Edward Dixon Abbott ran a motor-coach body-building business just outside Farnham in Surrey. As well as his core business he built gliders as well as those replica primitive flying machines for Korda's film. He also knew people in the aviation business and so it wasn't all that much of a surprise that Abbott's got the job when the *Daily Express* newspaper, having gallantly agreed to pay for the rebuilding of Appleby's now-even more aeronautically-challenged Flea (they were still hell-bent on a sponsored tour).

With the collaboration of ace glider-builder Leslie Everett Baynes, Abbott and Appleby got their heads together and, with hindsight realised what had been wrong. As a result, Baynes recommended two important changes. First was the substitution of a main wing of seven metres' span and second was a new engine. The 'thirties engine entrepreneur Sir John Carden had already been working to modify the basic ten-horsepower Ford motor engine for aircraft use. He needed an aeroplane to try it in and saw Appleby's fractured Flea as a golden opportunity. He offered to make a conversion for Appleby's second version of G-ADMH.

Crucial to this modification was the provision of dual ignition (two sparking plugs per cylinder) which modification alone increased the power from a dubious 22 brake-horsepower to rather more than 30. A light-alloy crankcase sump also saved some weight – not a lot but at that end of the power scale every ounce was a help.

The rebuilt and redesigned Flea was promoted as *The British Pou* by Abbott and Baynes. It was a great success and Appleby flew it all over the place, even taking it to France to meet again with Henri Mignet.

Meanwhile, the Baynes and Abbott duo were still enthusiastically thinking through the whole Flea concept, in particular the business of controlling the angle of incidence by pulling on a wire and relying on an elastic cord to keep the wing in position on the ground. Appleby's aircraft was modified to try out a rigid linkage to move the wing. It worked.

Not surprisingly, then, the Farnham duo carried on with ideas to improve the aircraft. Now came a bold move indeed. Forming themselves into a 'firm within a firm' as Abbott-Baynes Aircraft, the two men projected a wholly-new Pou, this one not only with the wing incidence controlled by a rigid connecting rod but with compensated controls to lighten the stick loads. A pair of railway-signal-style circular iron balance weights were attached to arms that formed part of the control column-wing pivot so that the wing was correctly poised.

Abbott's new Flea also had a proper strut-braced wing. Oddly, in view of the wing struts, they named it *The Cantilever Pou*. It flew very well and attracted wide attention. Initial rate of climb, very poor in the original Flying Flea, was now around 300 feet a minute and the aircraft was impressively manoeuvrable. So successful was it that Abbott-Baynes Aircraft laid down a production line at the Wrecclesham workshops of E D Abbott Ltd and soon had six machines almost complete save for engines.

Meanwhile across the country Fleas were being built and flown with varying degrees of success. Aiding its expansion were two main events, the first being Britain's first-ever Flying Flea Rally held at Ashingdon in Essex on April 13th 1936. Next came the Grand Flying Flea Trophy Race staged that August Bank Holiday at Ramsgate's brand-new Municipal Airport.

At this time Sir Alan Cobham's National Aviation Day tours were giving displays up and down the land. Rival 'air circus' was C W A Scott's touring team. Both decided to follow the modern trend and add the Flying Flea to the fleet of aircraft which operated the events. Quickly, though, both operators realised that the Flea was not up to this sort of operation calling for the strict adherence to a schedule of events and cross-country distance flying between. Both circuses dumped their Poux after a couple of months.

A Fatal Flaw

There was, however, a simple but fatal flaw in Mignet's 1935 design and this was the method in which the centre of gravity was established by moving the front wing forwards or backwards. With an aeroplane of common or conventional layout this is a harmless exercise and, as we all know, actually works rather well – but with the HM-14 Flying Flea there was a nasty side effect. If the front wing had to be moved too far back to get the balance right, then its trailing edge increasingly overlapped the leading edge of the rear wing.

The outcome of this was that as the pilot pulled the stick back to climb, the incidence on the front wing increased, ever-narrowing the gap between its trailing edge and the leading edge of the rear wing. Frederick Handley Page had patented just such a device back in the 1920s: it was called a slot and the effect was to generate increased lift over the wing it was applied to.

In simple terms, the harder the pilot pulled back on the stick, the greater the lift over the rear wing so tipping the aircraft forwards. It was a form of control-response reversal that would catch out novice pilots and experts alike.

At the same time, if the stick was pushed forward, there was a tendency for the aircraft to perform a half-bunt and end up inverted in which position it proved stable.

Because the engine mounting of the *Flying Flea* was not easy to move forward or backward, the only way to regulate the centre of gravity was by moving the wing. In general, heavier engines allowed the wing to be well forward, a situation in which the aircraft could fly extremely well. But there was no much flexibility in the allowable tolerances of building that this became a critical issue that was courting disaster. It was virtually inevitable that sooner or later somebody would be caught out.

On April 20th 1936, the first British fatality occurred when G-ADVL powered by a 34 hp Anzani inverted Vee twin motor weighing 112 lbs, dived uncontrollably into the ground. Built in Glasgow by R H Paterson, the crash at Renfrew on April 20th 1936 killed pilot A H Anderson.

It was when two highly experienced pilots were killed – the Air League's own test-pilot Flt.Lt A M Cowell in R G Doig's Anzani-powered G-AEEW, and Sqdn.Ldr C R Davidson, CFI of No.2 FTS Digby, in his own Flying-Squirrel-powered G-AEBS – that serious thought was officially given to the aerodynamics of the *Flying Flea*. By this time, four people had been killed in France and one each in Switzerland and Algeria.

Designed to the Mignet formula, the Croses-Flicot CF-1 Mini-Criquet F-PVQI was registerd in August 1974. This, the prototype, now rests in the Musée de l'Air at Le Bourget where this picture was taken in June 1981.

The Air League tries to Make Amends

As the body that had so strongly backed the Flying Flea in the first place, the Air League of the British Empire became very concerned that something was seriously amiss. It requested that the Royal Aircraft Establishment at Farnborough carry out an investigation. A full-sized Flea was placed inside the RAE's 24-ft wind tunnel in the late summer of 1936.

When the results of the evaluation were published, they were damning in the extreme. Report No.BA.1333 dated September 1936 was written under Air Ministry Reference 430302/35/DDSR by A S Hartshorn, BSc. Hartshorn would go on to become the RAE's principal scientific officer so he was well-qualified to make a pronouncement. His fulsome 10-page report drew the following conclusions. First was that the aeroplane was unstable in normal flight when the centre of gravity was further back than 0.4 of the chord and in a dive this instability became more marked. Second was that the control setting of the aircraft tested was a maximum of 4.8 which was only sufficient to give a positive pitching moment about its centre of gravity at angles of incidence down to -15°. At more negative angles of incidence, recovery could not be made. Furthermore a change of centre of gravity position of 14 centimetres made very little difference to the amount of control available.

The slipstream played very little part in recovery from a dive. In fact, if the aircraft entered a dive of -15° even with the stick hard back there was no possibility of normal recovery. Stability related to inverted flight at a speed of 50 mph – literally it preferred to fly upside down. In a dive, the machine entered 'unstable equilibrium' and curiously the position of the centre of gravity was more or less irrelevant.

This was a disaster for builders of Fleas, many of whom had already experienced the curious tendency of their aeroplanes to turn upside down, fortunately (for most) close enough to the ground to cause little or no injury.

While Mr Hartshorn was blowing wind across his charge at Farnborough, similar tests were taking place in the French wind-tunnels at Chalais-Meudon. Farnborough's findings were corroborated but the French went further, and finally came up with some recommendations to remedy the problem. The trouble, said the French, while very serious, was also very simple to cure. It merely required a fairly

In 1938 Mignet introduced his HM-16, a spruced-up variant of his earlier model. In New Zealand, engineer Robert J Germon of Ngatea, North Island, re-worked the design producing the HM-16/G. Built in 2000, ZK-FLE is powered by a 35 hp Cuyuna two-stroke engine and weighs just 320 lbs empty.

basic change in the Flea's formula to ensure that there could never be a slot effect to the rear wing. The British Air Ministry, however, was fed up with home-made aircraft and the bunch of retired Army colonels which infested Whitehall's corridors of power elected to adopt a far simpler remedy – it would not issue any more Authorisations to Fly and neither would it renew any existing ones. It wasn't a ban, it was simply a denial of existence!

While it may not actually have been a formal prohibition, it amounted to much the same thing as far as most people were concerned. When the news came in October 1936, it marked the end of the Flea craze in Britain. A few Fleas were built afterwards and these did fly successfully, but the boom days were at an end. Constructors across the nation, their hopes for cheap flying dashed, converted their handiwork into hen coops, tool-sheds – or kept them until November 5th and its fiery rituals.

As for Abbott's production line at the Wrecclesham coach works, Abbott knew he had solved the problem but he also knew that the Flea now had a reputation and that trying to market his version of the aircraft would be about as effective as endeavouring to poke a pound of warm butter up a porcupine's nostrils using a hot knitting-needle.

The news from the Air Ministry was received by telephone early one morning. Abbott stopped work at once and in a gesture typical of his nature offered the incomplete and engineless machines to any of his workforce that wanted one – at sixpence apiece! Older residents of Farnham recall the curious sight one lunch time of men dressed in Abbott's overalls gleefully pushing their prizes home, plywood suburban-dwelling gate-guardians that stood for a short while until they rotted or blew away.

The One that Got Away

But there had been a fourth fatality in Britain that September and many have linked this unfortunate event to the decision to 'ban' the aircraft. This aircraft, though, was powered by a Scott Flying Squirrel engine – a motor designed expressly for the *Flying Flea* and one with which the *Flying Flea* normally flew quite well. Admittedly it had been fitted to the fatal G-AEBS.

This one accident, though, has left behind it a large quantity of information and qualified eye-witness evidence that goes a long way to confirming that it was not entirely the fault of the aircraft. This evidence only surfaced again recently.

G-ADXY was built by a youthful garage proprietor named James Goodall. It was his second Flea: the first was not registered. Goodall's family ran a motor business at Echt in Scotland and the Flying Squirrel-powered 'XY was built in his spare time before being taken by road to the aerodrome at Dyce, Aberdeen. It was here that the *Flea* received its Authorisation to Fly in December 1935.

On March 13th 1936 the aircraft was flown for the benefit of the photographer from the local paper, the *Aberdeen Journal*. For this occasion the pilot was John Charles Neilan, an ex-de Havilland Aircraft Company pilot who had joined Aberdeen Airways as the company's third pilot (after James Gordon Hay) the previous month. Neilan, a highly-skilled and experienced commercially licensed pilot, went on to amass a number of pre-war gliding records.

Neilan's flight in G-ADXY was uneventful and afterwards he expressed himself in glowing terms regarding the machine's flight qualities. Who had carried out the first flight is not recorded but Goodall is known to have made a number of subsequent flights throughout that year, until the fateful events of September 20th. Watching that last flight was Neilan's friend, Eric A Starling, a highly-experienced airline flyer. As Aberdeen Airways' chief pilot he went on to complete a distinguished career with Gandar Dower Airways before joining British European Airways.

Goodall was seen to take off in G-ADXY and proceed to fly around without any problem for an estimated hour and a half when without warning the engine stopped at an altitude of about fifty feet. The aircraft 'drifted' down to about fifteen feet and then took a nosedive into a ditch. The pilot was not strapped in and was flung forward into the back of the engine sustaining severe head injuries. He was taken to hospital where he died three hours later, ostensibly the fourth death 'caused' by the *Flying Flea* in Britain.

The Inquest

At the subsequent enquiry, an amazing story emerged. Presided over by the Sheriff – a man with the splendid name of Alexander James Louttit Laing – an Aberdeen jury heard how 34-year-old James Goodall met his death solely through his inexperience.

This Sheriff's inquest found that although there was still fuel in the tank, the design of the fuel system was such that starvation would occur when a certain level was reached. But the official enquiry went on to turn up several unexpected additional details that came as something of a surprise to all concerned.

First was the revelation that the late Mr Goodall had had no flying training whatsoever and that his total time on the Flea was just two hours. The enquiry greeted this news with understandable astonishment. Furthermore it was discovered that the aircraft had never been subjected to official inspection at any time, the authorities at the airport having unwisely assumed that possession of a valid civil registration and third-party insurance was proof of airworthiness! This came as an even greater shock to John Neilan who told the Sheriff's court he had no idea the aircraft had not even been inspected by a qualified engineer and simply took it for granted that it was, as he put it, 'certified'.

In recording a 'formal verdict', the Jury recommended that any Flying Flea 'ought not to be permitted to be flown unless it has been officially tested, and a Certificate of Airworthiness granted by the Ministry', and that 'no-one should be allowed to pilot [the aircraft] unless a certificate of competence [the 'A' Licence as it was called in those days] has been obtained.'

Eric Starling concluded that the stoppage of the engine confronted the pilot with a situation that his absence of proper pilot training denied him adequate opportunity to cope with. In other words, the poor fellow hadn't a clue what to do. He probably attempted to maintain himself in the air by hauling further and further back on the control column until the front wing stalled as the lift over the rear wing increased. This nose-dived him into the ditch.

In truth, the ditch was probably an irrelevance since hitting the ground nose-down while not strapped in could easily have resulted in sufficiently severe impact injuries to kill him.

The Cruellest Cut

That September, while the Farnborough trials were in hand, the difficulties of the *Pou-du-Ciel* were brought home to its designer in France in a forceful way. Engaged in his own series of trials to find a cure for the aerodynamic peculiarities of his aircraft, a programme of test-flying some modifications ended in tragedy when Mignet's long-standing friend and business partner Robert Robineau entered an uncontrollable dive and lost his life. Robineau had built the second HM.14 and had been Mignet's demonstration pilot ever since. Nobody was more skilled at Flea flight than was he.

Mignet went to the United States, settling in Glenview, Illinois. Here, in the summer of 1937, he designed and built a new Pou which he called the HM-20. This differed from previous machines in having a higher front wing pivoted much further forward (about 22 percent of the chord) and the wing rigidly tiltable by a fixed-length rod.

But Mignet did not stay long in America, the impending war taking him back to France. He now entered a quiet period that was exacerbated by the war and personal tragedy which stalked him right to the moment of peace. Then he went to South America and finally to Casablanca where he eventually died, building aeroplanes to the end.

If the 1934-35 *Flying Flea* was an aircraft with a narrow margin of safety. Mignet ultimately learned from his errors and succeeded in evolving not just a solution but a whole series of subsequent variants on the *Flea* formula that have been wholly successful. Immediately after the war, he launched his HM-290 followed by the improved HM-293 and these heralded the start of a whole new family of machines.

Fleas Abroad

Flying Fleas resulting from Mignet's book quickly sprang up in other parts of the world, perhaps nowhere stronger than in Japan where Nihon Hikoki K.K (which translates as Japan Aeroplane Company) applied for a manufacturing licence from Mignet in 1935. Suitably equipped, the firm laid down a production line of 25 machines (they called it the NH-1 Hibari or Skylark) of which fifteen were licensed before news of the European restrictions caused a cease of operations.

Aside from the rash of Poux which enveloped France, Canada also saw a number built including at least one on skis. New Zealand had founded its Pou-du-Ciel League in 1935 and at least twelve projects were started before news of the French restrictions curtailed efforts. Even so, three examples were registered under the unique 'ZM-' series and at least two others flown. In post-war years, a further example of a later design has been registered ZK-FLE built by Robert J Germon of Ngatea, 50 miles south-east of North Island's Auckland.

But it was in Australia where the greatest number of Fleas were built outside Britain. This was in spite of extremely strict Australian airworthiness rules (stricter even, at that time, than ours) which virtually prohibited any aircraft from flying without a full and certifiable Certificate of Airworthiness. Happily Australians, like Yorkshiremen, don't respond easily to city-dwelling rule-makers and so the first flight of Flea built by Henry and Howard Rudd with Horace Roberts on January 31st 1936 at Box Hill Golf Links outside Melbourne was reported in the press but did not provoke official repercussions. The Rudd Brothers' unregistered Flea was fitted with a 48 hp Blackburne Thrush three-cylinder engine and could become airborne in just 50 yards.

On June 1st, the Australian authorities issued a circular categorically prohibiting all further flying of Fleas. Six weeks later a second Flea was tested at Parafield Airfield and the following May another was flown with a Blackburne Tomtit Vee twin. A further example flew with a 600cc single-cylinder Panther engine, perhaps the only single-cylinder-engined aircraft ever flown. Most, however, used the Clancy-Watt Henderson engine conversion.

In all, at least 56 people are known to have been actively involved with the Flea in Australia before 1939. Of these up to a dozen are thought to have been completed, half that number are known to have flown with varying degrees of success and, according to Meggs (*Australian-Built Aircraft & The Industry*, 2009), another three are presumed to have done so.

Unblemished Revival

Henri Mignet remained in touch with me for some years, his last card showing the sprightly-looking HM-300 three-seater with engine-cowlings arranged to look like a smiling face – a typical gesture of the irrepressible Mignet.

There are still aircraft being built to the Mignet 'formula' and today there survives the company he founded. Now run by his sons and family, it has new types of Flea such as the HM-1000 Balerit and the HM-1100 Cordouan.

If one wants to sum up the achievements of this affable Frenchman then, with deference, one might quote from Christopher Wren's own testament on being asked where his memorial was to be found: 'look around you!' he said. For Mignet achieved something unique. He sowed the seed of amateur aviation at a time when it didn't exist.

To say he brought flying to the masses would be stretching fact. In America, popular magazines had serialised plans for amateur-built aircraft so the genre was not entirely unknown – save in Europe. Mignet's solution was neither ideal nor adequately thought through. His engineering was intuitive and his aerodynamics rather too much error and not sufficient trial, but the point is that in his own way he succeeded and he flew himself the way he wanted to.

While he may not have been the poor man's aeronautical Messiah, he was very much a stimulus. He altered peoples' mind-set. Perhaps more accurately he convinced ordinary folk that if you put your mind to it then anybody really *could* build and fly an aeroplane.

For all his failings, his contribution has now been cemented in history: in March 1999 he was posthumously elected to the Experimental Aircraft Association (EAA) Homebuilders Hall of Fame. Britain has yet to honour him.

It was actually the legacy of his inspiration that brought half a dozen enthusiasts together in 1946 and resulted in the formation of the Ultra Light Aircraft Association – today's Popular Flying Association (now called the Light Aircraft Association), counterpart of the Experimental Aircraft Association in America and the Réseau du Sport de l'Air in France not to mention similar bodies in Australia and New Zealand.

Yes, Mignet took the arcane aspect of aviation and threw it away leaving only the part that mattered – the bit about soaring like a bird. And that should be Henri Mignet's lasting epitaph. All amateur aviation owes him an immense debt of gratitude for without his first steps on the road to home-building, the path would have been much, much harder.

And it was more than 75 years ago that it all happened.

Mignet's formula up to date! The HM-1000 Balerit is a Rotax-powered tandem two-seater with folding wings. The all-up weight is 450 kgs. C-IDBF was built in 1998 and imported into Canada in 2004 where is now belongs to Gerald De Gosbois of Quebec.

If Mignet is remembered for his *Pou-du-Ciel*, or *Flying Flea*, we should not forget that there were numerous other designs that paved the way to that aeroplane which set racing the hearts of budding aviators the world over. Here is a rare picture of a Flea precursor, the HM-8, the prototype of which was designed and built in Henri Mignet's Paris apartment and tried out in 1932. This curious hybrid aircraft had conventional rudder and elevator controls but the ailerons were merely 'pull-down' surfaces returned by elastic chords to their normal positions. Here is an example photographed by Henri Mignet himself and built by his life-long friend Albert Mouchet of Paris. Mignet commented that the aircraft was underpowered with its Tudion motorcycle engine.

After the very public failure of one of his early designs at Paris's Orly Airport, he decided that all his future experimental work should be undertaken well away from the eyes of both the general public and his fellow aviation enthusiasts whom he knew were sceptical and critical of his goals. Accordingly he toured the countryside on his elderly motorbike to find a quiet spot. Here we see Henri Mignet at work at his camp site in the woods at Soissons in the summer of 1931. Left is the motorcycle combination behind which he towed his aircraft and to the right is a forerunner of the Pou-du-Ciel, the HM-11 triplane powered by a twin-cylinder Harrissard 500cc motorcycle engine fitted with home-made 4:1 reduction gear. The woods and open spaces may have had a sanatory effect on Mignet yet he must also have known that were he to have a serious accident, outside help was not on the agenda.

After his first successes with the HM-14, he immediately sat down and wrote his book *Le Sport de l'Air* – hand-written with his own sketched-out drawings. It sold by the thousand and enthusiastic Frenchmen responded to Mignet's clarion call that anybody – everybody – could build their own aeroplane. A very early disciple of Mignet and his Poux was garage proprietor André Lordel of Feuquières in the Somme area of Picardie in Northern France. Here he poses with his Pou and, as many a true Frenchman still does when pictured with his aeroplane, his mascot – a top-wing toy monkey. The engine is the 25 hp Poinsard. The undercarriage displays some original thinking.

With its 17 hp Aubier et Dunne engine, this French-built HM-14 illustrates the pre-war design to perfection and also shows one the Flea's less-practical aspects – the sharp leading edges to the wings. Later designers would go to great trouble to ensure the optimum – but adequate – radius of their leading edges. Mignet's airfoil for the Pou-du-Ciel was arrived at experimentally.

At this time, French homebuilt aircraft were not required to carry registration markings and this HM-14 is seen flying at Orly in October 1935 in the hands of Henri Mignet. The distinctive form of the aircraft is well illustrated in this picture. While some refer to it as a tandem-wing aircraft, purists prefer the more precise (if pedantic) pigeon-hole of 'a tailless super-staggered biplane'. Either way, it seemed to be the answer to the layman's prayer – a cheap and easy-to-build aeroplane which did not require well-honed skills in order to build, and which could fly behind a converted motorcycle engine. What could go wrong with that!

In England, the first person to be bitten by the Flea bug was one Stephen Villiers Appleby. He had spent some time in France and had met Mignet and now decided that he would introduce Mignet's wonderful aeroplane to the British. For an engine, he took a normal water-cooled Ford car engine and radiator and bolted it onto the front of G-ADMH. It was extremely heavy but the advantage was that, having four cylinders, it ran very sweetly and quietly and was almost completely free of the vibration associated with a twin-cylinder motorcycle engine. Appleby assembled his first HM-14 Flying Flea at Heston. Here he poses in it beneath the shapely lines of G-ACZP, the Jersey Airways' DH.86 *The Belcroute Bay*. The ungainly single-ignition Ford 10 motor with its rear radiator right in front of the pilot's face restricts forward view. Standing by the engine wearing the trilby hat is the tall figure of Sir John Carden who would subsequently re-work the engine into the well-known Carden-Ford that powered a number of subsequent Flying Fleas as well as the tiny Chilton Monoplane. The DH.86 survived the war and was owned by Viv Bellamy at Eastleigh until a heavy landing at Madrid cracked the centre-section mainspar and rendered it beyond economic repair in September 1958. And later that day, in front of the press photographers, Appleby would fly his handiwork.

Appleby's aeroplane stands ready for flight. With the wisdom of hindsight it is easy to see that this short wingspan version was virtually doomed to failure thanks to the huge and aerodynamically-challenging application of a standard motorcar engine with its coil ignition, battery and cooling water. While smooth-running and quiet to operate, complete with radiator it weighed the best part of four pounds per horsepower. Most aircraft engine of the time were just over half that.

A smiling Stephen Appleby poses with everything ready for the official first flight before the cameras at Heston on Monday July 29th 1935. It was a warm and windless day – and he was now only moments from disaster. The power output of the basic Ford 10 engine was uncertain but it was promoted as 10 horsepower. Brake tests suggested 22 bhp but that was still a tiny number of small horses for such an enormous weight of engine and drag.

Just beyond the outskirts of Heston Airport Stephen Appleby's pride and joy lies inverted in a newly-harvested potato-field. Appleby escaped disappointed but otherwise uninjured. The mainspar of the wing has clearly snapped from the weight of the aircraft and its engine at the primary pivot-point. In those days the Automobile Association also took pains to look after the interests of private fliers and here we see a helpful AA man in uniform and cap confronting what may well have been his first aeronautical challenge: how to turn an upside-down Flea back on to its wheels! *Flight photograph.*

Stephen Appleby's Flea is carefully picked up after its abortive flight. All the oil has poured from the engine onto the underside of the top wing. The pilot, although shaken and covered in the black stuff, was unhurt. In the distance, Heston's large gas-holder stands as airport guardian and chief hazard. Photograph by *The Aeroplane.*

The rebuilding of Stephen Appleby's Flying Flea, paid for by his sponsors, the *Daily Express* newspaper, was undertaken by the Farnham-based coachbuilders E D Abbott, a company run by a decorated First World War RNAS pilot, Edward Dixon Abbott. The firm had already built gliders and would go on to make the replica early flying machines to be used in Alexander Korda's dreadful movie *The Conquest of the Air*. Now, with the help of sailplane designer Leslie Everett Baynes, came the first re-working of Mignet's design and the replacement of Appleby's original Ford engine with a neater installation of a Carden-Ford aircraft converted car engine. Here is the so-called British Pou being erected in the company's coachworks at Wrecclesham. It was a very different aeroplane, even if the registration letters were the same. *Picture by courtesy of C R Shepheard.*

Now painted up with details of the engine, G-ADMH is ready for flight once more – a wholly-new aeroplane but with an already-flown registration. The two slack cables to the aft of the wing are the control wires that move the wing about its front-spar pivot point. The wing, when at rest, is supported by a telescopic strut at its trailing edge. When in flight, the wing is restrained by the control cables which become tight. The name 'The British Pou' is displayed prominently upon the rudder together with the name and address of Abbott-Baynes Aircraft Company Limited.

The rebuilt Flea exhibits a number of improvements. Apart from the increase in wing-span to seven metres, the fuselage structure was altered to provide a proper bearing for the engine mounting. This provided a vital forward attachment point for a drag bracing wire connected to a pivot bracket on the underside of the wing spar which also provided anchorage for parallel wires to the upper surface of the rear wing. This overcame a lack of torsional stiffness detected in the original airframe and shown by a tendency for the two wings to 'fan' slightly under load. This also allowed a large parallel cut-out to be provided with a door for cockpit access. Above all, the dual-ignition Carden conversion of the Ford motor-car engine was fitted with its neat, drag-reducing radiator located in the underside of the nose. The apparent 'tub' on top of the wing directly above the engine is Heston's famous gasometer in the distance.

The silver and red Carden-powered Abbots-Baynes rebuilt G-ADMH running up prior to flight. This view shows very clearly the neat installation of the engine and its systems with the cowling vents to take away the cooling air after it has passed through the radiator. Forward visibility, however, was only slightly better.

The rebuilt G-ADMH Flying Flea takes off from Heston's grass in the presence of the photographer of the weekly magazine, *Flight*. On October 9th, 1935. The large and drag-inducing radiator is now mounted less obtrusively under the engine and enclosed within the snub-nosed front fuselage.

Shortly after trials began with the new G-ADMH, an important modification was carried out that formed the interim version of what would become the Abbott-Baynes Cantilever Pou. This was the deletion of the telescopic wing-support strut and the replacement of the rather untidy loose control wires to the front wing by a rigid control rod that supported and moved the wing without 'backlash'. This formed the third incarnation of G-ADMH seen here in flight at Heston.

With a broad smile on his face, the goggles-and-helmetless Appleby does a low pass for the benefit of the camera, his expression indicating the success of the Farnham engineering company's work. The success of the 'Farnham Flea' would inspire Abbott and Baynes to look even further ahead…

The *Daily Express* newspaper sponsored an extensive tour of Great Britain by Henri Mignet and his Flying Flea. The tour began at Shoreham and went to many coastal and provincial towns. It was at the Bournemouth venue that the author first met Mignet and his Flea. The rest, as the saying goes, became history! Here is the much-travelled Flea overnighting in a wooden hangar. Note the long exhaust pipe trailing almost to the tailwheel from the Aubier et Dunne engine. The colour scheme was Mignet's own style and was copied by many, not the least his friend and fellow Flea flier, Robert Robineau.

While all this was taking place, Henri Mignet was working on his next designs. The man never seemed to stop working and within months came the HM-18 which would be the star of the forthcoming Ramsgate meeting of 1936. But before that – or possibly concurrent with it, Mignet introduced an even smaller machine which he styled the HM-16. It was known as the Baby-Pou or miniature Flea. In recent years this has been reworked by Georges Jacquemin as the HM-160. This picture reveals the diminutive size of this practical looking insect. Notice, incidentally, the rounded wing leading edges and the rigid push-rod-operated main wing. Both of these changes suggest that something had made the designer aware that the HM-14 airfoil was neither efficient nor tolerant of sharp alterations to the angle of attack. From what seems to have been a decision to avoid the number thirteen in his designs, Mignet always gave even numbers to his designs: those later ones appearing with odd numbers were individual versions of his originals such as the HM-293.

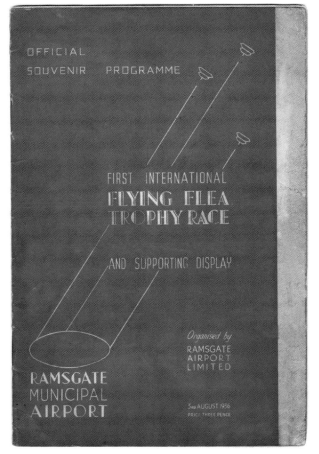

OFFICIAL SOUVENIR PROGRAMME

FIRST INTERNATIONAL

FLYING FLEA TROPHY RACE

AND SUPPORTING DISPLAY

Organised by
RAMSGATE AIRPORT LIMITED

RAMSGATE MUNICIPAL AIRPORT

3rd AUGUST 1936
PRICE THREE PENCE.

In Britain, the newly-opened Ramsgate Municipal Airport staged the first-ever Flying Flea Trophy Race on the August Bank Holiday 1936. Organised by British Flea-builder Stephen Appleby, although the French came over in force only some eight machines gathered on the grass. While I was only a very small boy, I knew that some history was beng made that day. Here is the cover of the programme which I have carefully kept for all those years

The title page of the 'Grand Air Display' on August 3rd, 1936. It was hoped to attract 'huge numbers' of Fleas and the promoters actually expected to have to stage heats to keep the number of machines in the 'final' down to a practical number. Such precautions were not necessary as it turned out. The race began at 4 pm and was run over four laps of a seven-mile course between the airport and RAF Manston. There were three prizes totalling £200 and a cup. Engine starting proved the major stumbling-block and in the end there were just six starters. The race was won by Frenchman Edouard Bret in his 27 hp Ava-powered Pou, Britain's Stephen Appleby came second in his *Daily Express*-sponsored rebuilt Flea Mk.II with its purring four-cylinder Carden-Ford engine, and the third place went to Mignet's friend and collaborator, Robert Robineau behind a 17 hp Aubier-Dunne twin-cylinder two-stroke. It was a good day out but even with Henri Mignet present to add authority to the event, most of the flying was undertaken by other and more conventional machines such as Aeroncas, Cierva Autogiros, a BAC Drone and a joy-riding Monospar.

The Ramsgate gathering produced this visitor, a French-built HM-14 powered by a 17 hp two-cylinder inline Aubier et Dunne engine. Later, a three-cylinder version of this engine was developed which gave 27 hp at 3,200 rpm. With a total capacity of 810cc and built-in reduction gearing of 2.05:1, the propeller speed was 1,600 rpm. A novelty was that each cylinder had its own carburettor and fuel pump, not something that would delight all but the most ardent engine-tuner. As far as is known, only Mignet himself flew with this engine in a Pou.

Highlight of that event in Kent was the latest design of the master. Henri Mignet had quickly produced a cleaned-up cabin version of his Pou-du-Ciel which he called the HM-18. It was powered by a 32 hp Moteur Mengin air-cooled flat twin. The insignia on the rudder shows a rising sun with a line of Flying Fleas emerging. Note the connecting rod to move the 'living wing' (Mignet's term). The designer was never afraid of using long, thin push-pull rods operating at angles that might make better engineers gulp.

The crowds that visited the new Ramsgate Aerodrome were greatly impressed by the appearance of Henri Mignet in person flying his latest machine, the HM-18. It flew extremely well and was clearly so much better than the HM-14. British Pou pioneer Stephen Appleby of G-ADMH fame bought this aircraft and registered in G-AENV but he took it back to France late in 1936 when he moved there.

With cabin top, decent undercarriage and a skid in place of the HM-14's twin tin tailwheels, this aircraft was both faster and aerodynamically superior. With such a powerful engine, this Flea had a very impressive performance.

Here Henri Mignet and Stephen Appleby discuss details of Mignet's new HM-18 during the Ramsgate Rally in 1936. The Mengin engine was a popular and lightweight French aeromotor also used in the Avion S.C.A.L. FB.30 Bassou G-AFCD (and later in my own Luton Minor before being replaced by an Aeronca JAP). Noticeable here is the aerofoil-section fuel tank which formed the filler for a large rectangular hole in the wing of this Flea variant.

A feature of the Ramsgate Flea meeting was that the public was not dissuaded from taking a close look at the aeroplanes on show. Here a young man takes a close interest in the Moteur Mengin on the front end of Henri Mignet's visiting HM-18 while another is watching the aerial cavorting taking place as incidental attraction to the greatly anticipated Trophy Race for Fleas.

While the events of that distant August were taking place, concerns over the safety of the Flea were mounting and within a month, serious trials would be conducted in the big Farnborough wind-tunnel. But for the present the frantic Flea activity would continue unabated. Here is a close-up of the 22 hp Aubier et Dunne engine of the Flea that was about to become the Air League's Air Commodore Chamier's personal runabout based at RAF Hendon.

The post-war aeronautical cartoonist 'Polkm' characterised the poor Pou as an oddity made out of half a tin bath and an orange-box – and ever underpowered! Here is his 1950s cartoon, originally published in *Popular Flying*, the journal of the one-time Popular Flying Association.

The persistent problem with homebuilt aeroplanes seems to have been the choice and availability of suitable engines. The little Douglas, ABC and Bristol motors, while ideal, were too costly for most builders, so they tended to turn to more familiar sources for their engines. Here is a close-up of the Austin Seven engine in Charles Cooper's G-AEEI. Built in Surbiton, this HM-14 was well-engineered but suffered from the extreme weight of its engine which, with radiator and cooling water, was rated at only 13.5 horsepower. However, the engine was mounted very low on the nose so only the chain-driven reduction gearing to the propeller really obscured the pilot's vision. The radiator, reduced in size, was mounted on the port side of the nose. In all, it was a well-thought-out conversion which was competently carried out. The price, while low in pounds sterling, was high in pounds avoirdupois.

A standard French-built HM-14 revealing the method used to mount the engine. Since each motor required a different system of mounting, it was left to the builder to decide the best form of attachment. This appears to have involved ad hoc engineering relying on the principle of MLTJ (More Luck Than Judgement), especially since the main wing drag loads are transferred to the fuselage nose via the engine itself. The name Cyrnos might suggest that this machine was involved with a popular Parisian hotel.

Sir Alan Cobham's National Aviation Day Displays Limited toured the country giving popular air displays wherever they went. In the summer of 1935 it was felt that each of the company's two tour teams would benefit from the addition of a Pou and so Henri Mignet was invited to build two aircraft. In due course, these were delivered. Virtually identical, they were typical and standard French Pous but fitted with the 25 hp Poinsard engine rather than the less powerful usual motor which was the 17 hp Aubier et Dunne. The two machines were registered on September 11th, 1935, G-ADSC and 'DSD. It was quickly determined that the Flea was not a suitable aircraft to undertake the gruelling tour schedule and after two months it was willingly sold to the Scott Motor Cycle Company Ltd as a test-bed for its Flying Squirrel engine. It was withdrawn as 'cancelled' in December 1936.

G-ADSD, sister to G-ADSC, was likewise disposed of after barely a couple of months, the new owner that December being W G Bennett of Aldenham who kept it at the local newly-opened Aldenham Aerodrome, now called Elstree. He managed to crash it the following March.

A standard HM-14 Flying Flea built by A N Francis at an unknown location. The engine is a BSA Vee-twin of unknown power output.

Newspapers were 'aviation aware' in those far-off days. Unlike today when lightplane activities are thought blasé and not newsworthy, editors sought out aircraft stories and those featuring the small man in his workshop were sure-fire guarantees of a good picture story. And so when Fox Photos got wind of the fact that a man in Colchester who ran a garage had been asked to build an aeroplane, the agency photographer was around like a shot! Taken on January 31st, 1936, this shows a garage owner named Wilkins well on the way with his Flea which he was building for his customer, L V G Barrow, also of Colchester. For every Flea that appeared on the British register it is reckoned at least ten others were started. But this Flea was completed, becoming G-AEFE. It flew at Ipswich that summer but its return to Wilkins Garage proved unlucky: the garage burned down with 'EFE within.

G-AEBB was built in 1936 by K W Owen at Southampton and gained its Authorisation to Fly on January 24th that year. Powered by a 1,300cc four-cylinder in-line Henderson engine (the engine developed by American Ed Heath for his Heath Parasol) it is reported to have flown until it scared its pilot and was grounded. A colourful history followed which included ownership by an ATC Squadron before it was presented to The Shuttleworth Trust at Old Warden in 1969. By now it had lost its engine, a deficiency remedied by its new owners who found a Flying Squirrel to fit on the front.

A poor quality snap shot showing a historic moment in Blackburn, Lancashire, as Tom Proctor taxis his newly-completed British Anzani-powered Flea along the cobbled street while friends and family push and steer. Taken on March 19th 1936, the picture shows that Proctor's machine, one of the earliest to be finished in Britain, incorporated some interesting changes. The fuselage nose and undercarriage have been dramatically altered. He had started building the previous November and gained Authorisation to Fly on April 7th. Testing was carried out at Barton and apparently a total of nine flights was completed.

American record-breaking and stunt pilot Clyde Edward Pangborn (1895-1958) was the first person to fly the Pacific Ocean non-stop. Here he is pictured running the engine of the first Flying Flea to be seen in America. This was Mignet's own HM-14 No.8 which he took to the US in May of 1937 when he and his wife Annette went there to form the American-Mignet Aircraft Corporation. On December 11th Pangborn was invited to fly the Flea at Roosevelt Field, Long Island, New York. Unaccustomed to the individualistic controls, he made an unconventional take off (the press reported that 'the left wing came within inches of hitting the ground') but finally succeeded in making a circuit. His comments after landing were not recorded.

If Ramsgate, Ashingdon and Heston were the key Flea events and their places in Britain, the earliest in France was Orly, Paris, where, in the autumn of 1935, the French aviation magazine *Les Ailes* organised a Flea gathering. Technically, even in France, homebuilt aircraft were illegal but, thanks to that commendable national characteristic of constructive blind-eye approach to bureaucracy, the event went ahead, actually under the patronage of the then French Minister for Air! No wonder France became so great a nation not just in amateur aviation! The picture shows the unique Flea built by Francis Kohler and André Baumann. Apart from its 45 hp Salmson radial motor and increased wing span and dihedral, it also had an 'improved' and fully reworked fuselage, push-rod-operated wing and an undercarriage modified from a French fighter biplane. Here we see the pipe-smoking pilot striding purposefully out across wet tarmac at Orly in October 1935. The aircraft flew extremely well. *Picture by courtesy of Flight.*

Opposite: A mysterious picture of an unregistered Flying Flea taken (according to a note on the photograph) in the Princess Hall (no place but possibly Cheltenham). The name on the rudder is The *Fleeing Fly* but this is not the same as C L Storey's G-ADXS of the same name. The wing control system is a long, thin push-rod which makes a mockery of Euler's Rule, and the engine is unknown. The forward wing cabane struts have characteristic kinks around the windscreen. Nothing further is known of this example.

Charles M Cooper of Cooper's Garage, Surbiton, built G-AEEI in 1936. It gained its Authorisation to Fly on April 1st and was powered by a supremely smooth-running but desperately heavy Austin Seven car engine. This engine, which was rated at 13.5 hp, featured a chain-driven reduction gear for the propeller shaft. It was exhibited at Ashingdon in Essex on the tenth of that month (where this photograph was taken) – but was taken there by road.

Famous if only for its challenging paint-job, Joe Wood's black and white G-AEBT was built in his motor-business garage in Solihull. Powered by a Ford 10 car engine converted by Wood himself, it featured a 'chin'-radiator directly under the propeller hub. Unlike the Abbott-Baynes' installation of the Carden-Ford, this radiator was vertically mounted so giving the aircraft a pronounced bluff snout. This Flea was one of four built by a syndicate of friends in the Birmingham area, chief amongst which was the one-handed glider-builder Don Burgoyne whose own Flea G-AECN was famously inverted into a hedge by Wood. While G-AEBT was hopped a few times it never flew satisfactorily through lack of power. G-AECN's flying was much better: it had the lighter Scott Flying Squirrel engine and was also immortalised in an extremely well-photographed Gaumont Newsreel movie 'short'. After its later crash, the registration was re-used illicitly on the low-wing Burgoyne-Stirling Dicer, a JAP J.99-engined single-seater built from cut-down BA Swallow components.

June 10, 1936]   PUNCH, *or The London Charivari*   645

"YOU DID TELL ME WHAT IT WAS, DEAR, BUT I'M AFRAID I'VE FORGOTTEN—SOMETHING TO DO WITH INSECT POWDER, ISN'T IT?"

LA SOCIÉTÉ DES AÉRONEFS

HM. 19
BIPLACE-CABINE
DOUBLE-COMMANDE COTE-A-COTE

...vergure	6 mètres
...ngueur	4 m. 80
...ds à vide	240 kgr.
...ssance	45 C.V.
...on d'action	400 kil.

Performances

...collage en 70 m. (vent nul).
...ntée à 200 m. en 1 minute.
...art de vitesse 40-150 km. : h.

MIGNET

MEAUX (S.-et-M.) FRANCE
présente ses modèles
HM. 16 - HM. 18 - HM. 19

Ces appareils non encore connus du public français, dérivés de la formule Pou-du-Ciel 1934, sont d'une mise au point toute récente (nouveaux brevets déposés en France et à l'Etranger en 1935-1936). Ils vont être soumis à l'homologation internationale.

Leur principe nouveau d'aile *à fente commandée* allié à la stabilité du *parachute* permet de voler sans danger en **perte de vitesse** et rend impossible la *glissade* et la *vrille*, tout en leur assurant les performances des bons avions modernes.

Cette formule qui, seule, autorise d'aussi faibles dimensions, en a rendu la réalisation particulièrement **robuste et bon marché**.

HM. 18
MONOPLACE-CABINE

Envergure	5 mètres
Longueur	3 m. 60
Poids à vide	120 kgr.
Puissance	35 C.V.
Rayon d'action	400 kil.

Performances

Décollage en 60 m. (vent nul).
Montée à 300 m. en 1 minute.
— — 4.000 m. en 40 minutes.
Écart de vitesse 40-150 km. : h.

LES PLUS PETITS AVIONS DU MONDE
ÉCONOMIQUES ET CONFORTABLES

les plus sûrs

HM. 16
MONOPLACE-TORPEDO

...nvergure	4 mètres
...ongueur	3 m. 30
...oids à vide	100 kgr.
...uissance	25 C.V.
...ayon d'action	400 kil.

Performances

...écollage en 50 m. (vent nul).
...ontée à 200 m. en 1 minute.
...art de vitesse 40-130 km. : h.

les plus faciles à piloter

Henri Mignet, ayant obtenu du *British Air Ministry* l'autorisation de voler en Angleterre, s'y rend par la route et par le bateau et put offrir la primeur de son dernier modèle en vol au public anglais, à RAMSGATE, LYMPNE et LONDRES, et voler librement sur le territoire de Grande-Bretagne.

Attestations de la Presse spécialisée :

— « L'événement sensationnel du jour, pour les connaisseurs, fut la
» démonstration de M. Mignet avec sa nouvelle cabine HM-18. C'est
» un véritable POU-DE-CHASSE (*interceptor Flea*). Le décollage est meilleur
» qu'avec n'importe quel autre avion ordinaire et la montée se fait immé-
» diatement à grand angle. La stabilité latérale semble excellente malgré
» l'air agité et il effectue des virages à la verticale avec une étonnante
» fermeté, tandis que, hélice calée et parachutalement, ne décelant aucun
» vice caché, il évolue avec une parfaite confiance. » (*The Aeroplane*.)

— « Indubitablement, la démonstration la plus attractive de la journée
» fut celle de M. Mignet sur son nouveau HM-18 à haut rendement. »
(*Flight*.)

— « Le HM-18 a l'air d'un grimpeur parfait et d'une belle petite
» machine qui eut un gros succès à RAMSGATE. » (Hervé Lauwick
dans *L'Aéro*.)

— « Sauf les avions de chasse les plus modernes, je n'avais encore rien
» vu de semblable. Je ne comprends pas qu'on achète un avion monoplace
» quand on a vu voler le HM-18. » (Edward Bret dans *Les Ailes*.)

les moins chers

Vue aérienne de
l'AÉRODROME PRIVÉ
de la S. A. M.
à 40 km. Est de PARIS
MEAUX-ISLES-LES-VILLENOY
(Seine-et-Marne)

Société à responsabilité limitée. — R. C. Meaux 13.165.

An undated but clearly post-1936 leaflet published by Mignet following the Ramsgate meeting in which he expresses his gratitude to the 'British Air Ministry' which granted him special authorisation to fly in England – for its time this was an unprecedented relaxation of ever-more stringent rules and regulations that were well on the way to throttling amateur enterprise out of existence.

Opposite: The Flying Flea craze was at its peak in the early summer of 1936 and it was thus fitting that the weekly satirical magazine *Punch* should have a Flea-related contribution. Indeed, it was almost inevitable that sooner or later this fine periodical, so much a barometer of British life, would have some sort of reference to the fact that in a nation firmly rooted in traditions of horse-riding, lawn tennis and croquet, people everywhere were now besotted with aeroplane-building. It fell to one of the magazine's most respected senior cartoonists, Harold William Hailstone (1897-1982), to produce this Flea *dénuement*, for the aircraft was only months away from being the subject of a 'no certification' order. In Hailstone's cartoon, the lady tries unsuccessfully to recall what the pilot (possibly her son) calls the aircraft. What is apparent, incidentally, is that Mr Hailstone must have been quite familiar with the airframe of the *Pou-du-Ciel* for there are certain very precisely-drawn details that go beyond a cartoonist's ability to sketch in a representation of an object. The undercarriage, tailwheel and fuel-tank detailing is more than coincidentally precise.

The arrival of the Flying Flea in Britain was accompanied by a proliferation of small companies offering parts or prefabricated kits, among these being Grice Aerowheels, Luton Aircraft, Dart Aircraft, Aircraft Constructions. Carden-Baynes Aircraft, East Midlands Aviation and so on. Most were extremely small outfits, several being 'one-man bands'. But one or two set up as manufactures to produce and sell complete aircraft, usually characteristically modified from the original HM-14. One of these was Putnam; another was Perman who launched its version, illustrated here. Founded by E G Perman in 1935 expressly for producing Fleas, the business also produced its own modified Ford car engine that was cheaper than the Carden model. Originally it was to be called the Perman Poupower but somebody pointed out that this could be misspelled and misunderstood. The whole project proved an expensive mistake as did the firm's attempt to produce a follow-up 'normal' aeroplane – the Perman Parasol. The business disappeared by 1938. The Perman Flea was distinguished by its wide-span wings, vertical nose-mounted radiator and Abbott-Baynes-type wing push-rod control. Eleven examples were registered, not all of which gained clearance to fly. Here is one of those that did – G-ADPX.

Many small businesses – even individuals – joined in on the Flying Flea bandwagon offering to make parts and components. When *Popular Flying* published a special edition devoted to the Flea in November 1935 it secured supportive display advertising from plywood manufacturers, steel-tube makers, providers of dope, the Douglas aero-engine, and Whyteleafe Motors, conveniently situated between Croydon and Kenley aerodromes, advertised 'Complete machines, numbered parts or materials for immediate delivery'. There were countless others, too. Here, from *Flight* of July 16th 1936 is a notice from the small company Perman offering major assemblies at prices that, even allowing for the passage of time, seem astonishingly low.

One of the modified Fleas built by E G Perman in London WC1 was G-AECM fitted with a Perman-modified Ford engine. It was the eleventh and last Flying Flea that this firm made and it received its Authorisation to Fly on April 8th 1936,

C W A Scott's Flying Displays Ltd was based at Hanworth where it had constructed G-AEFK powered by a 30 hp Carden-Ford. A rival to the Flea flown by R G Doig for Campbell Black's Circus (this was the Anzani-powered G-ADPW), 'EFK displayed on its nose and rudder a richly-coloured representation of the character 'Bertie Bassett' advertising a well-known brand of liquorice 'allsorts'. The aeroplane enjoyed but a short life, being cancelled the following March.

This advertisement appeared in the magazine *Popular Flying* for November, 1935 and promoted Fleas built to the Baynes-revised G-ADMH.

After the rebuild of an improved G-ADMH for Appleby, the Abbott-Baynes business at Farnham evolved a whole raft of improvements to Mignet's design. The upshot was the so-called Cantilever Pou, a restyled Flea variant with strut-braced wings and a balanced control to the main wing in the form of a metal arm which carried at its forward end a lead weight. Here prototype G-AEGD is parked on the garage forecourt at E D Abbott's Wrecclesham Road forecourt – the old petrol pumps can be seen in the left background. This head-on view shows the robust wing support mechanism and, visible between the lower end of the lift struts and the fuselage side, the counterweighted arms of the wing pivot control system. *Picture by C R Shepheard of Farnham.*

With properly strutted wing supports, the Abbott-Baynes Cantilever Pou was a machine with more potential than the basic HM-14. Although the engine is still both rich in weight and drag while feeble in power, it is at least better cowled. *Pictured at Wrecclesham Road by C R Shepheard of Farnham.*

The prototype of the Cantilever Pou, G-AEGD, made its first flight at Heston in April 1936 with Appleby at the controls. In this second re-work of Mignet's HM-14 design, the single pivot-point for the main wing was replaced by two, the central cabane being deleted in favour of two outer pivots created by replacing the bracing wires with tubular lift-struts and an inverted broad Vee side cabane. However, a major problem was now found to be the relatively high stick forces required to move the wing. This was overcome by providing lead counterweights fixed to cranked arms attached to the wing actuating lever on each side of the fuselage. These were felt to be an interim solution but the movement of the wing centre-of-pressure across the flight envelope suggested little was to be gained from simply altering the pivot point of the wing. Very apparent in this view is the change in airfoil made by Leslie Baynes. Gone is Mignet's reflex upper camber in favour of a more conventional wing section. *Picture via Mike Hooks.*

This side-on view reveals the vastly-improved lines of the Cantilever Pou and displays the adjustable-length wing incidence control rods and the revised fuselage nose which affords a proper forward point to which the wing pylon struts may be attached. Visible just behind the wheel can be seen one of the two wing-balancing arm-mounted static weights.

Another view of the Cantilever Pou revealing the counterbalance attached to the control-column pivot for moving the wing.

Stephen Appleby runs up the Carden-Ford engine in G-AEGD on the grass at Heston prior to first flight. *Picture by C R Shepheard of Farnham.*

Following on the successful rebuild of Stephen Appleby's G-ADMH (which its creators were quick to dub 'The British Pou') the equally successful flight trials of the Cantilever Pou proved an inspiration to coachbuilders E D Abbott of Farnham. This business, founded by former RFC pilot Edward Dixon Abbott, had its works just outside the town in the hamlet of Wrecclesham on the road to Petersfield. It was here that glider and sailplane designer Leslie E Baynes had designed the aircraft to embody Sir John Carden's modified Ford motorcar engine – the 30 hp Carden-Ford water-cooled inline motor. Here G-AEGD is pictured by the *Flight* photographer at its first demonstration in April 1936. The plan was to put it into production with a sale price of just £150 which was about the average price for a family saloon car and around a third of the price of a 'normal' light aircraft.

Unlike the French who had cheap and suitable motorcycle engines that were easily converted for use in the Pou-du-Ciel, we in Britain were still lacking an affordable lightweight engine. The Scott Motorcycle Company of Shipley in Yorkshire identified a market for a small engine that would power British Flying Fleas. Already in production with its Squirrel motorcycle and twin-cylinder inline air-cooled motor, the company made the necessary changes to create an aeronautical variant which it called the Flying Squirrel. With a bore of 73mm, a stroke of 78mm and a compression ration of 6.1:1, the engine developed 28 hp at 4,000 rpm for a weight of about 85 lbs – a weight of just over 3 lbs/hp. A right-hand tractor, it would drive a five-foot diameter propeller having a pitch of 4.35 ft. The price was £50 plus £3 for airscrew hub and flange. The propeller

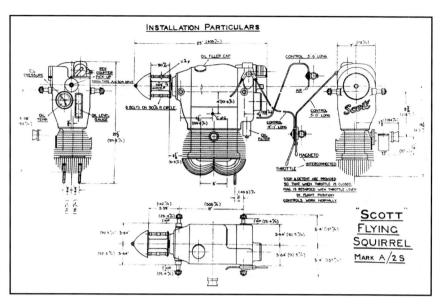

cost another six guineas - £6.6/-. A neat engine which made for a clean installation, this became the preferred motor – but human nature being what it has always been, it did not prevent constructors from trying to fit just about anything that they had to hand from a variety of motorcycle engines to converted motor-car engines, mainly Ford but also Austin in origin.

The Scott Company's design team had the prototype aero engine completed in the late autumn on 1935. In order to air-test it, the company bought a Flying Flea, G-ADSC, and fitted the motor to it. This particular aircraft had first flown that September with a Poinsard engine. Flying Squirrel flight trials took place at Yeadon Aerodrome on Saturday and Sunday, November 16th and 17th, in the hands of Flt.Lt Ambrose M Cowell who would later lose his life in R G Doig's G-AEEW the following May 4th. Pictured here in the rain after the first successful flight, from left to right, Alfred Holt (test engineer for Scott's Aircraft Engine Division), test pilot Cowell, Welham Cull (designer of the engine), Scott's marketing director and, far right, R A Vintner, Scott's managing director and registered owner of the aeroplane. In all, not more than about fifty aero engines would be built. *Picture courtesy of the Woods Archive, Bradford.*

One of the first new aircraft to be fitted with the Flying Squirrel was G-ADPP built by Cyril Brooke of Huddersfield. This machine gained its Authorisation to Fly on September 25th 1935. This actual picture became the publicity photograph used by the Scott company for its engines. Very heavily retouched and with the background removed, it showed a long exhaust pipe and silencer plus a picture of the absent owner carefully pasted into the cockpit. The photographer, C H Wood of Bradford, made a name for himself with his skills at creative photo-montage and adjustment done in an age long before computers brought such deception into the hands of the masses. *Author's collection via Woods Archive.*

The self-same picture! Here is what appears to be Mr Cyril F Brooke of Huddersfield sitting in his finished Flea. It is, however, a remarkable piece of studio fakery. Photographer C H Wood, has managed to impose a seated builder in the cockpit, remove the cluttered background – and fit a silencer to the engine! And all this almost 70 years before Photoshop and a computer makes this sort of thing commonplace. Bearing that in mind, one is still tempted to offer the comment 'just didn't he do well!'

Don Burgoyne's Knowle-built G-AECN pictured at its first roll-out in a rather wet back yard at the beginning of February 1936. The registration has yet to be painted on. The constructor is seated in the cockpit dressed for the part. The Scott Flying Squirrel engine is new. *Picture via Andrew Marfell.*

This is a particular type of photograph which, for those of a certain age, whispers ever-fainter memories of halcyon days when the sun always shone, the grass was ever green and the birds sang with abandon. It is a typical provincial back garden in Rishworth, West Yorkshire pictured in the summer of 1936. Parked on the lawn is S O White's Scott Flying Squirrel-powered Flying Flea. Never registered, it remains uncertain whether this example ever flew in which case it would be one of the estimated two or three dozen completed but 'illegal' Fleas that flew particularly in the North of England.

Among the lesser-known Flea-makers was a firm called East Midlands Aviation Company of Northampton. G-AEGV was built by them and test-flown at Sywell on May 24th, 1936, originally with an 850cc Douglas engine. After a wartime career with the Air Training Corps (ATC), it was restored by the Midland Aircraft Preservation Society at Coventry and fitted with a Scott Flying Squirrel. Taken on occasional tour, it was pictured here at Greenham Common on Sunday July 8th, 1973.

G-ADXS was built in Southend by Christopher L Storey and powered by one of the new Scott A2S Flying Squirrel in-line inverted twin air-cooled engines. The aircraft, named *The Fleeing Fly*, gained its Authorisation to Fly on December 4th 1935 and survives today in preservation.

A pair of revealing views of Christopher L Storey's Southend-built G-ADXS. This shows to good advantage the relatively enormous size of the rudder and the geometry of the wing incidence control push-rod. He started building this in August 1935 and completed it that November, gained its Authorisation to Fly on December 4th, and completed its maiden flight at Rochford on December 15th – surely a record for building an aeroplane.

In this view of G-ADXS one can see the dangerous proximity of the trailing edge of the main wing to the leading edge of the rear one. It also displays clearly the curious reflex upper curve of the Mignet wing-section or airfoil. Compare this with the Abbott-Baynes Cantilever Pou on page 45. This particular machine was resurrected after the War, displayed at Southend from October 1959, and is now in an aviation museum.

Begun in January of 1936 and built to the plans published in the magazine *Practical Mechanics*, G-AEFE was built at Colchester by a man called Wilkins for the registered owner, L V G Barrow, also of Colchester (see picture on page 36). The engine was a Scott Flying Squirrel. It underwent tests at Ipswich that summer but early on it sustained some damage. It never flew again for, soon after this picture was taken showing the largely unfulfilled attempts at starting the engine, the garage in which it was stored burned down.

Constructed by E G Perman Ltd for E H Chambers, Scott-powered G-ADPY got its Authorisation to Fly in February of 1936 and was initially based at Heston. It had a revised undercarriage with compression struts rather than the original low-slung bungee-sprung pivoted axles.

The intrepid aviator returns to earth after a long day's journey. Flown by the Air League's chief test pilot Flt.Lt Cowell, the Scott Motorcycle Company's G-ADSC, flying test-bed for the company's new aero engine returns from a test flight. It is Sunday, November 17th, 1935, at Yeadon Aerodrome. *Picture by C H Wood.*

Pictures of Fleas in flight are not as common as those showing them posed safely on the ground. This may have had something to do with the fact that the control responses could be unpredictable: Joe Wood, who built and flew G-AEBT in Solihull with Charles Vaughan, recounts how on one landing attempt he was suddenly confronted with some sheep but, on sharply pulling back the stick to climb over them, he found himself diving upside down into the ground. Fortunately he was uninjured but it was a salutary lesson that while some Fleas flew well if left alone, sharp control movements often led to unexpected results. Here, however, Flt Lt Cowell flies the Scott-powered flying test-bed G-ADSC across the expanse of Yeadon Aerodrome. *Picture by C H Wood.*

A rather poor snapshot of Don Burgoyne's Flea on roll-out day at Knowle and yet to have its registration, G-AECN, painted on. The Scott Flying Squirrel engine was rated at 34 hp at 5,200 rpm – far too fast for an efficient propeller. It was usually operated at 4,000 revs which produced about 28 horsepower. Burgoyne built a number of aircraft and, during the 1939-45 War, rebuilt training gliders for the ATC. All this was the more remarkable because he only had one hand and even that was mutilated: as a 14-year-old boy, he had been playing with a shot-gun and had stood it, butt down on the ground. Now with both hands folded over the muzzle, it suddenly discharged, blowing off Burgoyne's right hand and leaving his other with several fingers missing. Burgoyne went on to complete a career as a skilled aircraft carpenter and, as an accomplished pilot, flew many of his own creations.

While the winter of 1935-36 was, for the greater majority of British Flea builders, devoted to construction, the end of winter brought realisation to many a project. Some were lucky and their Fleas flew reasonably well. Others had a host of problems most of which ended up in crashes, the majority of which, fortunately, hurt merely pride and pocket. The Knowle-based Flea construction club built around the talented Don Burgoyne was not to escape the Flea jinx. His example first flew that February but on March 15th Don's G-AECN managed to get airborne in the hands of Joe Wood when it suddenly dived into the inverted position landing in a hedge against a tree. It was observed that it had managed to fly perfectly level upside down but could not be righted. Miraculously Wood escaped serious injury and took this photo as the inevitable gathering of spectators gawped. The indefatigable Burgoyne took his broken aircraft home where it was rebuilt and back in the air that May.

The Knowle jinx continued as the local Flea squadron suffered another mishap. On April 16th, L E Mottram's G-AEFI hit the ground extremely hard at Leamington, miraculously without injury. A 2/6d Box Brownie (127 film size) recorded the event as light failed.

Don Burgoyne's restored G-AECN was rebuilt unaltered. Nobody seemed to realise that in recreating it exactly as before, whatever its problem was would remain. That May he had a more serious crash, again upside down. This time Joe Wood, who was a member of the unofficial Knowle group of Flea builders, was heavily concussed. This terrible snapshot is the only one known to exist of this terminal event. Those registration letters would, though, be re-used. Don went on to build a low-wing monoplane incorporating parts of a BA Swallow and fitted with a JAP engine. He called it the Burgoyne-Stirling Dicer and it was unofficially painted as G-AECN. The Air Ministry knew nothing about its existence! It was still around – and flying – in the 1950s.

Amongst the many personalities who were associated with the Flying Flea was a remarkable GP from Anstruther in Fife, Dr Matthew D S Armour. In the early part of 1936 he wrote to Luton Aircraft Ltd, then of Tatling End, Gerrards Cross in Buckinghamshire, and ordered a kit of Flea parts. Luton Aircraft had been set up by Cecil Hugh Latimer-Needham expressly to supply parts and kits for the Mignet machine. The company also handled Anzani engines – a motor which the firm would later modify for its 1938 Luton Minor design. Dr Armour assembled his Flea and fitted the 30 hp Luton-supplied inverted Vee twin. He completed it by October 1936 and registered it G-AEOJ with flight trials initially from Scone but, immediately after the Air Ministry report, he felt it prudent to transfer flying to a large field three miles north-west at Carnbee. In 1937, he modified the undercarriage to provide better springing and, crucially, better ground clearance. At the same time he arranged the rear wing to pivot. In this photograph, Dr Armour stands by the rudder of his machine with a pilot friend at Carnbee. With the outbreak of war, the aircraft was put into store but its ultimate fate is uncertain. Dr Armour is remembered as an accomplished watercolourist but his main contribution was as a breeder of budgerigars: his definitive book on the subject remains in print.

It is unfortunate that numerous authorities (including A J Jackson in his *British Civil Aircraft 1919-1972*) described G-ADXY as claiming the life of its builder when it 'became uncontrollable and crashed'. This is simply not true. Although builder/pilot James Goodall had no formal flying training, let alone a pilot's licence, and although his aircraft had never been inspected for airworthiness, it nevertheless flew extremely well as testified by leading commercial pilot John Neilan who flew it and enjoyed the experience. Goodall was killed when he ran out of fuel and, never having been taught how to handle such then-fairly commonplace emergencies, did the best he could but ran into a ditch. The thing that killed him was not the Flea but the fact that he was not wearing a seat-belt, let alone a proper harness, Here James Goodall stands by his Scott Flying Squirrel-powered G-ADXY at Dyce in Aberdeenshire. In the background can be seen the airport terminal building and the hangar.

Close-up of 20-year-old James Goodall running up the engine in his home-made Flying Flea G-ADXY on a very cold March day at Dyce. Nobody knew at this stage that Goodall had never received a flying lesson in his life, nor had the aircraft received any airworthiness inspection. It would shortly be making its first flight at the hands of one of Scotland's most experienced airline pilots.

It is March 13th 1936 and Goodall's Flying Flea takes off on its first flight in the hands of John Charles Neilan, third pilot of Aberdeen Airways based at Dyce. Here the event is pictured by a photographer from the *Aberdeen Journal*. Neilan's verdict was that the aircraft flew well and was sprightly in the very cold air.

Neilan pilots James Goodall's G-ADXY through the Aberdeenshire skies quite unaware that the machine has neither been certified as airworthy nor even checked by a competent engineer. All that would come out soon afterwards when the inquest into the death of the young Goodall, who had no pilot's licence but had taught himself to fly his own Flea the way Mignet unwisely recommended, revealed the extreme irregularities of this Flea's flights. But Goodall was not killed by the Flea's perversity; because he lacked the security of a seat-belt he was thrown forward and smashed his head on the back of the engine.

Because of the radio-telephony 'Q' code, combined with the potential of visual confusion between 'O' and 'Q' (which has never bothered the French), since G-EBTQ issued in August 1927, British registrations have avoided the letter 'Q' altogether. Additionally, those with the power to issue registration letters have always been reserved to the point of being thought prudish when it came to groups of letters that could be 'misinterpreted'. This means they stoically resist entreaties to issue certain other letter groups that might be thought rude, risqué or ribald. One that crept through, though, was the *Evening Standard*'s Westland Sikorski helicopter which was allocated G-ANAL due, it seems, to the powers giving consideration only to the potential for three-letter groups rather than four: having got a Tiger Moth down as NAL, they seemed to have learned a lesson by the time the 'A' series reached RSE. Which is why the register is free of aircraft marked BUM, SOD, TIT and so on. And the Air Ministry never issued 'FFI', aware of the interpretation amongst Servicemen. To generations in uniform, 'FFI' meant 'Free From Infection', a welcome result for the recipient and usually written down on a medical report after a particularly embarrassing inspection often involving use of a pencil. One thus admires the humour of members of the Yorkshire Aeroplane Club which built this accurate replica of a Flea and with a sang-froid well-matched to our French friends, boldly painted it with the never-issued and thus forbidden letters.

The cover of a celebratory booklet produced on the Pou-du-Ciel by the French magazine *Les Ailes*.

Flying Flea G-AEBA had a curious history that culminated in this rather poor picture of it upside down amidst the corn-stooks. Built in 1936 at St. Teath, Bodmin in Cornwall by A Oliver, it carried the builders' reference A.O.1 and was powered by an Anzani inverted Vee twin. The registration was cancelled a year later in 1937 and the aircraft 'disappeared', only to turn up almost three years later 53 miles to the East at Kennford, Exeter. It was just weeks after the outbreak of the 1939-35 war which combined with a late harvest when a nameless pilot decided to get G-AEBA running, whereupon he embarked on a series of fast taxiing runs up and down a field, presumably just for the hell of it. It was stated that he had no intention of taking off but, having applied full throttle in order to turn the aircraft round after one run, the throttle jammed wide open (so he later said). Not that this was a totally unheard of thing with this engine thanks to the mechanics of its Amal carburettor. If the throttle cable was very slightly slack (stretched), when in the fully-open position the soldered nipple could slip through the side slot in the throttle control lever on the carburettor leaving the cockpit occupant no alternative but to cut the ignition switches. On this occasion, the pilot must have panicked for he quickly became airborne, flew across a small but deep valley and met the rising ground of the cornfield on the other side. As the clouds of war broke over Britain, the final pre-war Flea lay wheels uppards in the Devonshire stubble.

This is the 'Flea' that Claybourn's built. That's what it said on the rudder of G-AEKR built by E Claybourn Company Ltd of Doncaster. It differed from other fleas in having a rounded bottom to the fuselage and (like many others) a non-standard rudder profile. Powered by an Anzani inverted Vee twin, it was completed by June of 1936 and first flown at Doncaster by R Parker on May 28th, 1936. In total it made just four flights, the last being on June 23rd 1937. It was stored during the war parked in the roof trusses of a garage as shown in this picture. Subsequently it was given to RAF Finningley where it was accidentally destroyed in a hangar fire on September 5th 1970.

Preserved today is this reproduction Flea comprising original wings and other parts and provided with a spurious registration, G-AEOF. It is otherwise a genuine machine. Note the elastic cords attached to the engine bearers and the top wing used to stop the wing flopping down over the cockpit when on the ground.

What the pilot sees from a Flea cockpit, namely a pretty good close-up of the back of his engine, in this case the Scott Flying Squirrel. This is the installation in G-AEOF. Note the revolutions counter attached directly to the rear of the engine.

Begun in 1935, G-AEEH was constructed in Bath by E G Davis and completed with a Scott A.2S Flying Squirrel engine. It made its first flight at Whitchurch on November 5th 1936 – after the Air Ministry had announced that it would issue no more Authorisations to Fly for Flying Fleas. This example is said to have performed a number of successful short-flight 'hops' before being relegated to storage. Like a fair number of Fleas, it survived the war and is now preserved in the RAF Museum at St Athan in Wales where it has resided since 1076. Today it appears to be fitted with an incomplete engine of indeterminate origin.

By the middle of 1936, it was painfully obvious that the Flying Flea had hidden problems that were beyond the classification of 'pilot's finger-trouble'. The Air League was in the unenviable position of having avidly sponsored the Pou-du-Ciel in Britain. No less a luminary than Air Commodore John Adrian Chamier, CB, CMG, DSO, OBE, had endorsed the Air League's translation of the French book: he even owned his own Flea, G-ADME, which he kept at Heston. Now there was a rising tide of accidents that all seemed to point to the probability of inherent instability. And now there were fatalities. After its own highly-qualified test pilot Flt.Lt Ambrose Malcolm Cowell had been killed in G-AEEV on May 5th, 1936, the Air League requested help from the Air Ministry. It wanted a programme of basic stability trials to be run on a Flying Flea in the large wind tunnel at the Royal Aircraft Establishment, South Farnborough. G-AEFV was lifted into place in the throat of the tunnel, the propeller removed and a dummy pilot seated in the cockpit. Tests were carried out under the scrutiny of the leading aerodynamicist A S Hartshorn at a simulated airspeed of 65 mph. It was Thursday August 13th, 1936 – an auspicious day for the HM-14 Flying Flea in Britain.

How the Flying Flea was supported in the wind tunnel for the Farnborough tests in August 1936. The cockpit is occupied by a life-size and weight dummy. Beneath the chamber can be seen the laboratories in which various readings and calibrations can be taken. The office on the right is that of Arthur Stanley Hartshorn who was the author of the report published the following month. These trials to some extent mirrored those taking place around the same time in France although it has to be confirmed that the French trials were considerably more extensive and investigated a wider area of the Flea's performance envelope.

By the end of the 1939-45 war, the Flea, while still closely recalled by most people, was considered history. The RAF hosted the *Daily Express* 'Fifty Years of Flying Exhibition' at Hendon Aerodrome between July 19th and 21st, 1951. This big display coincided with the Royal Aero Club's Jubilee celebrations so it was the event of the decade and was graced with the presence of many aircraft. While most flew in, some had to come by road. Among this group was G-AEHM, the Flying Flea in the collection of the Science Museum. Built by H J Dolman of Bristol and powered by a Douglas flat twin motorcycle engine, it flew at Whitchurch on May 2nd, 1936. In September the same year, the constructor responded immediately to the Farnborough report and donated his handiwork to the South Kensington Museum. Years of storage has taken its toll: one blade of the propeller is broken.

Always a good attention-grabber at aeroplane shows are the naked ladies who bare their all for the close inspection by the curious of all ages. Here is one such attraction, most probably a newly-built model to show visitors how aircraft are built. It also serves to show the highly idiosyncratic Mignet wing section with its sharp leading edge and reflex upper profile.

Christopher Storey's Fleeing Fly, looking as good as new, sits silently in the Skyfame Museum of the Southend Historical Aircraft Collection. Note that this example has the Abbott-Baynes-type rigid control rod to the main wing although it lacks the counterbalances fitted to the later Cantilever Pou.

Canada was the first country outside France to get caught up in the Flea craze, largely because a major part of it was French-speaking and therefore had immediate access to Mignet's book. In all ten Fleas were completed and appeared on Canada's civil aircraft register. Probably the first built and flown was CF-AYM built at St. Hubert in Quebec and fitted with a ski undercarriage. Another was CF-BII powered by a Blackburne Thrush while CF-BIH had a Poinsard motor and was named *The Spirit of Canada*. Probably the most photographed Canadian Flea was also the one that didn't fly. Toronto's Central Technical School built CF-AZD but after the Farnborough report in 1936, the Canadian Department of Transport issued a similar edict to the British saying that it would not issue any Authorisation to Fly.

Here is a rather poor but rare picture of CF-AYM dating from about March of 1935. It was constructed in Montreal by Dr George E Milette and on March 2nd it was flight-tested by the Canadian Air Regulations district inspector, Stuart Graham. His report was that the aircraft was fine and the aircraft gained its Authorisation to Fly. The Flea flew well for more than a year apparently without problem until one unfortunate day at St. Hubert when it suffered engine failure on take-off. It was July 2nd, 1936, and the Ski-Flea dived into the ground and was destroyed. Miraculously, the pilot, E T Webster, stepped out unhurt.

In New Zealand, the authorities allocated a special national registration prefix for Flying Fleas. In place of the usual 'ZK' designation, the letters 'ZM' were reserved exclusively for the Mignet aircraft. Three were registered – ZM-AAA built by E Roy Perkins & Leonard Hawke at Waipukerau and fitted with a Douglas Dryad engine; ZM-AAB powered by an ABC Scorpion III; and ZM-AAC headed up by a Scott Flying Squirrel. This last aircraft was built at Oamaru by William L Notman and is preserved today in the Ferrymead Museum of Science & Technology, Christchurch. This picture is of ZM-AAB built by Richard D Downey and Allan McGruer at Mangere in May 1936. Downey is about to swing the wood. The aircraft was burned in 1950. At least four other Fleas were built in New Zealand but not registered. One, built by Angus Denize at Waikawau Bay, was tested on the beach as late as 1947 but crashed on its first flight attempt. Another was built and flown at Christchurch, its aerial endeavours also ending with a crash, and there were at least two others.

Another of the three New Zealand-built Fleas that were registered, this one the Scott-powered ZM-AAC which was built at Oamaru and was the most successful of all the Flying Fleas built there. Constructed by William L Notman, it was reported to have been flown at the township's Alma Airfield early in November 1938 by David Whitaker. During one of some eight flights undertaken, Whitaker is reported to have reached 1,000 feet, hopefully AMSL [above mean sea level] – parts of this delightful South Island seaside town soar to a giddy 265 feet above sea-level… This aircraft is today on display in a museum collection – but with the wrong wheels.

Another view of ZM-AAB built in Auckland by Richard D Downey and Allan McGruer. The engine was an ABC Scorpion. The aeroplane, apparently fitted with motorcycle wheels, was burned in 1950.

A Belgian-registered HM-14 Pou-du-Ciel, OO-07, showing a much-modified undercarriage and what looks like a Bristol Cherub engine. The owner, E Vérvers, poses with his creation at Brussels in 1937. The name, painted on the fuselage side, is *Oh! Mum!*

Another nicely-engineered Belgian Pou is pictured here. The engine appears to be a Harley-Davidson fitted with a chain reduction gear, unusually (for a Flea) fitted with a smart chain-guard.

Henri Mignet seemed in general unbothered by the reports of mishaps to his Pou-du-Ciel around the world. This attitude changed dramatically during 1936 after the fatal accident to the Pou-du-Ciel of Robert Robineau, his friend and chief collaborator. Mignet must have felt that he wanted to distance himself – literally – from the scene so in 1937 he went to America and settled in Glenview, Illinois. Here he designed a new Flea – the HM-20 fitted with a Continental A40 engine. The wingspan was 16 feet 7 inches, length 13 feet, height four feet five inches and the empty weight 425 lbs. Maximum all-up weight was 610 lbs and the fuel capacity was 12 US gallons or fractionally under 10 Imperial gallons. He was assisted in the construction by Frank Easton who went on to develop the aircraft. To protect the Mignet reputation, he renamed the aircraft the ME2Y. This picture shows the Easton-Mignet E-1, N13384, parked outside its hangar while those around are attracted to something in the sky above.

Mignet returned to his home country for the years of the war where he seems to have successfully exploited his Flying Flea design as a military observation machine with the advantage that it could be folded up and towed behind a vehicle. With the coming of peace, Mignet seemed revitalised despite the loss of his wife, Annette, killed by snipers during the conflict. Now Mignet launched a new design in her memory. *Le Sport de l'Air* was revived not just for France but the whole of Europe and anybody else who wanted to join in. The first notification of a potential Flea revival appeared in Britain in the summer of 1946 when advertisements like this began to appear in magazines. Whatever happened in continental Europe, there was no possible hope of any being built and flown in the British Isles. We had no legislation to allow them. More to the point, perhaps, we had no suitable engines either.

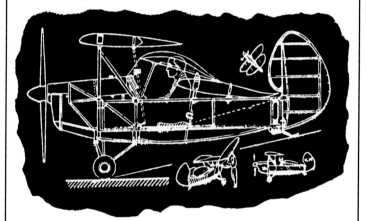

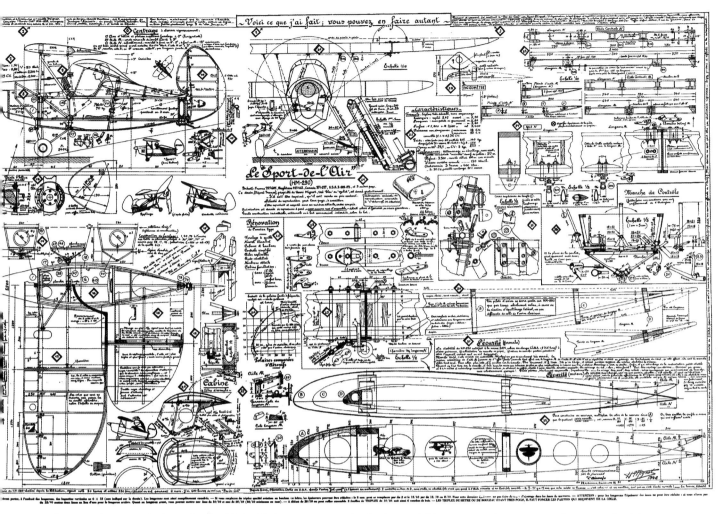

Here is the complete 'set of plans' for the HM-290 drawn on one single sheet of thin paper and presenting the novice builder with his first challenge. Complete with multi-language translation sheet, the price to Great Britain was just five shillings.

The post-war '290' and '300' series of Poux-du-Ciel featured one significant difference over the pre-war models – folding wings. This rather poor (and heavily retouched) snapshot shows how the Flea could be folded even smaller.

Henri Mignet's visit to America in 1937 saw his HM-20 design built with the help of a young Frank Easton. On Mignet's return to France, Easton continued to revise the HM-20, restyling and reworking it until he changed its designation to the ME2Y. This elegant and practical Flea's finest times were in the 1950s and 1060s when it was demonstrated regularly at the Experimental Aircraft Association's annual Fly-Ins. With the registration marks N43993, this Flea variant was developed to a very similar standard to Mignet's own HM-290 and HM-293 in Europe. Easton's Flea proved safe and practical to fly.

Frank Easton was America's most devoted Flying Flea fanatic and his boundless energy put the aircraft on the map there. Pictured at Rockford, Illinois, in 1965, this American built HM-293 Flea, N43993, put up a first-rate flying display. Notice the rear wing trailing-edge flap and the short-span main wing.

HM-293 Flying Flea N43993 running up for take-off at Rockford, Illinois, at the EAA (Experimental Aircraft Association's) annual Fly-In in 1965. Despite a great deal of interest, it is thought few Fleas were built in America, largely because they were too small for the huge distances pilots needed to fly.

Jean-Daniel Allard's HM-293 was built in 1947 at the time when there was uncertainty as to whether the registration would be a standard 'F-W' or one of the new 'F-P'. The indecision is reflected in the manner in which his allocated letters, 'FKA, were painted. But this Flea fell on hard times and is pictured here wings folded and engineless parked in the roof girders of its hangar. The reflex trailing edge of the rear wing shows up from this unusual viewpoint.

French amateurs very frequently stamp their homebuilt aircraft with their individual ideas. F-PYHD is actually an HM-293 although it would be hard to recognise it. Styled an HM-293W (the 'W' being the builder's initial), it was built in November 1979 and features a tricycle undercarriage, revised wing bracing and a large fixed fin. It was pictured at Popham on the occasion of the Henri Mignet Flying Flea meeting at Popham Airfield in August 1995.

Another view of the HM-293W showing the rather industrial nosewheel mounting and the converted VW power unit.

While the majority of Flying Fleas were single-seaters, the HM-380 was a side-by-side two-seater. Another Pou-plane from the hands of Albert Baron of Marennes, F-PKFB was the fourteenth machine to be built to this style and was registered on July 30th 1961. It was destroyed in an accident on May 18th 1969. This picture shows the style of cabin-top used on most post-war Fleas and shows how it lifts up and backwards. The long control rod to tilt the front wing is clearly seen here.

F-WKFK/F-PKFK was built in the summer of 1961 by Christian Martin of Calais as a HM-293. In the summer of 1965 it was sold to Belgium becoming OO-32. The engine is a VW conversion. Curiously, while it was Belgium that sponsored the Flea's post-war revival, only 21 Fleas ever appeared on the register – and a number of those were imported from France. How many examples were actually built and completed in Belgium is unknown.

Nevertheless it was France where the post-war years demonstrated the great revival of the Pou-du-Ciel. Here, large numbers appeared. So vast was the uptake of amateur construction in that country aided by designs such as Jodel, Turbulent and many, many others besides the Flea, that the French authorities were forced to create a whole new registration category for homebuilts known, phonetically, as 'Fox Papa'. Many aircraft previously registered in the usual civil series of 'F-W---' now found themselves forced to repaint as 'F-P---'. Here we see the former F-WFRH (yes, that fourth letter is an 'R') repainted with the old registration just showing through the otherwise superlative paint job. Built in 1946 and flown that July by the renowned (and prolific) French home-builder Albert Baron at Rochefort, it was originally a HM-290 but later up graded as a HM-296 in September 1956. Here it is powered impressively by a Salmson radial.

Originally built in 1956, F-PGYA is a HM-293 built by Jacques Hildebrandt of Mitry. At the time of writing, this long-term Flea is still airworthy and is flown by its current owner from Etampes. In this view it is pictured with the wings folded. Note the non-standard but effective side-hinged cabin-top. This machine is fitted with a rear wing trailing-edge flap (introduced by its inventor, the Swiss Flying Flea engineer and designer Louis Cosandey) extending over the fixed centre-section. It was Cosandey (1874-1941) who independently analysed the problems of the Pou-du-Ciel and worked out a practical solution which he published for the benefit of all other Flea builders.

In Britain, a post-war resurgence in Flea activity was rather stifled largely due to the effects of the six-year moratorium imposed on amateur aviation by the war. People's vague recollections of 'the banned aeroplane which killed many – even hundreds' had become transformed from myth first to assumption, then probability, and finally into hard fact by the passage of time. As late as 1955, a home-built aeroplane was, to the majority of ordinary folk, a Flying Flea – and these things were dangerous! The pre-war restrictions had likewise been turned into a full-blown ban and so much as mentioning one of these was to lay oneself open to ridicule. One man, however, took on the myth, legend and confusion and built himself an HM-293. Registered G-AXPG, W H 'Bill' Cole's Chelmsford-built Mignet design first flew in June 1971 having been registered on October 14th, 1969. Powered by a 1,300cc VW engine, the wingspan was 18 feet 1.75 inches, length 12 ft 6 inches, and empty weight 421 lbs. Maximum all-up weight was 643 lbs. The aircraft cruised at 80 mph, had a top speed of 91 mph and a range of 320 miles. It survives in store today.

Not all Fleas survived grounding in pre-war times and the majority were to suffer the brief but bright fate of a Guy Fawkes bonfire celebration. With the notable exception of the Science Museum's G-AEHM, it is really only in post-war times that the sanctity of the museum has been available to lucky candidates. When Bill Cole's VW-conversion-powered HM-293 G-AXPG was pensioned off, it found such preservation. This picture shows the underwing locks to the wing hinges that characterise both the HM-290 and its larger variants. This feature has created something of an airworthiness stumbling block for these designs as far as the British authorities are concerned. Although both front and rear spar breaks are united by hinges, only the mainspar hinges have locking pins which means that the integrity of the wing and its resistance to bending loads is only maintained by the mainspar. It does, however, all seem to work and the French have not complained about it.

The improved model of the HM-290, the HM-293, appeared in 1947 and, like its predecessor, was a robust, practical and popular flyer. F-PKFK, was built to the 821st set of plans sold and registered in August 1961. Built by Christian Martin of Calais, it was sold to Belgium in June of 1965 where it became OO-32 in the amateur-group registrations. The engine is a converted VW. As all those designers who sell sets of plans will have discovered, most buy plans out of curiosity: only about one in fifty actually cut wood.

Sitting quietly with its wings folded, HM-320 F-PHZI rests at the back of a hangar. Constructed in May 1957 by the Société Henri Mignet, then in Casablanca, it was restored by his son, Pierre Mignet, in May 1974 and twenty years later was consigned to the Musée de l'Air. This picture shows the wing hinges as well as the locking pins on the mainspar locations and nothing for the rear spar. The engine of his machine is a VW conversion and the undercarriage compression struts carry non-standard shock absorber fairings.

Described as being the property of the Société Henri Mignet of Casablanca, F-PHQT is the July 1956 prototype of the HM-351 two-seater. Mignet's Pou designs of this period had fixed cabin tops and cockpits that were accessed by decent-sized conventional hinged doors. Unless the windsock is fresh back from a starch-rich laundry, it must have been a very windy day.

In June of 1959 Henri Mignet introduced his latest Flea, the single-seat HM-360. Here is the first example to be built by Louis Gancel at Lessay. The engine is a 65 hp Continental air-cooled horizontally-opposed flat-four. The pitot head for the airspeed indicator protrudes from the wing leading edge: one wonders if it is both far enough forward of the overwing airflow and far enough away from the propeller slipstream to offer a reading with acceptable position-error. Like its predecessor, the HM-290, this has folding wings.

Mignet's HM-360 first flew at St.-Lô in France during June of 1959. Here is one fitted with what appears to be a Scott Flying Squirrel engine quite nicely cowled. The enormous tailwheel probably gave a smooth ride on rough grass but somehow spoils both the lines and poise of the aeroplane.

Businesslike in appearance and a far cry from the HM-14 of 1935, this view of the HM-360 F-WKFC shows it to be powered by a 65 hp Continental flat four. It reveals just how much Mignet had learned in the space of a quarter of a century. Perhaps most important was that he had taken notice of the science of the airfoil and chosen a wing section that had definable, measurable characteristics. Note the non-standard 'demi-cabin-top'.

Built by Albert Baron in the summer of 1961 this HM-360, the fourteenth made, was a perfectly standard model built according to Mignet's plans. The legend on the rudder reads 'A.B.08' (telling us it was the eighth aircraft Albert had built), 'Le CoLiBri' (indicating the aircraft's name) and then 'Aeroclub du Bassin de Marennes'. Originally it was operated on a full French authorisation to fly as F-WKFB, and later on restricted permit as F-PKFB. It was destroyed at Soute on May 18th 1969.

Pictured at Popham in August 1995, F-PFKC is the re-registered incarnation of F-WKFC illustrated earlier. Now with a different paint scheme, this is a classic example of a HM-360. As serial number 1, it was owned by Louis Gancel at Lessay in 1959. Passing through several different keepers, it has been systematically upgraded. The tailwheel, virtually attached to the rudder pivot, allows very precise, direct ground manoeuvrability.

Pierre Willefert built this HM-360 No.18, F-PNUO, at Pont-s-Yonne in the summer of 1972. The cabin top was hinged and opened backwards over the rear wing on parallelogram pivots to allow unrestricted access and exit. Note the neat sprung and swivelling tailwheel.

The first HM-360 to fly in America was Ralph M Wefel's N360HM built at Canoga Park, California. Here it is seen on November 25th 1962 being shown at a local fly-in 'in the white'. After a long flying career, it now reposes in the EAA's Museum.

A particularly smart-looking HM-380, the 64th built, was F-PMEP built in 1964 by Pierre Couradeau of Chauvigny. It was a fine example of the amateur craftsman's work. Its Authorisation to Fly expired in July 1976.

Developed from the HM-380, the HM-381 made use of a revised wing-tilt system employing a shortened push-rod pivoted at the fuselage top longeron position. F-PLUJ, originally F-WLUJ, was the 51st machine of its type to be made, this one constructed by Guy Roy at Chatellerault and first registered in December 1963. For a while it was owned by Mignet's son, Pierre Mignet. Note the curious tall tailwheel illustrating the individual quirks that were introduced by Pou builders.

The cantilever spring steel undercarriage of this two-seat HM-380L, F-PMET, gives this machine a contemporary, practical appearance that is stylish while at the same time low on drag. Built in September 1965, it was rebuilt in 1995 and remains airworthy today.

French aircraft builders have always been good honest experimenters in the correct sense of the word. For them, the latest trends and technologies were not to be shunned or overlooked. In this fine example of the HM-380L- the first built – we see the handiwork of François Lederlin of Grenoble. Dating from September 1965, F-PMET had a welded steel tube fuselage allowing a very large access door. The swept fin and rudder and steerable sprung tailwheel suggests a transatlantic influence while the sprung cantilever rod undercarriage shouts the work of the veteran US racing pilot and lightplane designer, Steve Wittman of Oshkosh. His W.8 and W.8L Tailwind might just have played a tiny part in this evocation of the Mignet theme.

A rather non-standard HM-390, F-PJXI, was the fifth to be built. As a modified HM-380, this has a welded steel tubular fuselage allowing large, step-in cabin access. Registered in June of 1961, it was built by Félix Eysseric of Visan and is now preserved in the Musée Pou du Ciel at Marennes.

The Pou-du-Ciel has always had a strong following in Belgium and here is a modern tricycle-undercarriaged Flea, registered 59CKF, pictured flying over water. Built by master woodworker Pascal Recour, it has a converted VW engine and took its builder ten years to construct. Finished in 2008 and named *Vogelfrit* 2, it was a star exhibit at the third Belgian Flea Rally staged at Cerfontaine Aerodrome at the end of August 2010.

The war left its mark on Henri Mignet: his wife was was shot right right at the end of the conflict. In 1947 he went to Argentina at the behest of friends and while there designed a three-seat cabin version of the Pou-du-Ciel. This was a large machine powered by a 125 hp Continental flat-four close-cowled with a chin air-intake that looked like the smile of a manic monster. Mignet shaped and painted the cowl to represent eyes and the hint of whiskers. He sent me this card in August 1949.

En recuerdo de nuestra encuentra
agradable en un mundo nuevo
a H Fonder
H Mignet

August 1949

The obverse of the picture card seen in the previous illustration. Mignet, born in 1893, was above all an aircraft enthusiast who perhaps naively believed that he had something to give to the world that the world really wanted. He was misjudged, mistrusted and maligned for most of his life and yet it is through his devotion and leadership that we have the amateur flying movement of today. Future generations please note! While France and the USA have accorded him posthumous tributes, Britain has ignored his contribution.

No survey of the Flying Flea would be complete without looking at other related designs – those inspired by Mignet's work and, perhaps, those who sparked the genius in Mignet himself. Let's start with a designer who, as a fellow Frenchman, may well have given Mignet the idea for two big wings and no tail. Peyret Taupin Type VI No.10 was registered to the Aero Club at Caen in May 1965 as F-PMEM having originally been F-APGB. Peyret had been foreman at Louis Blériot's aircraft factory before branching out on his own to develop his ideas based on his 1922 glider, surely an inspiration for Henri Mignet. On January 23rd, 1923, Alexis Maneyrol had set up a world record duration flight at Vauville, remaining airborne for eight hours and five minutes. Maneyrol's death in October that year at Lympne took a talented flier's life in his 32nd year. But Peyret continued with his ideas, initially with Pierre Mauboussin, from 1928 up to the time of his own death in 1933. His work was continued after his demise by Mauboussin and others. The enormous Taupin was the climax of a series of large aircraft that emerged from the design bureau Peyret had set up in 1928. In the 1970s this aircraft was to be seen around La Ferte-Alais but at the end of 1972 it was re-registered for the third time, taking the markings F-AZBG. Here it is showing off half of its eight individual lift struts.

The Mignet formula saw the evolution of other designs based on the Pou-du-Ciel. Here is a Croses LC-6 Criquet, the third example built. Designed by one of Mignet's leading disciples, Emilien Croses, this elegant two-seater design was followed by another similar but far lighter design called the Pouplume having a weight of just 65 kg. He went on to design and build some fifteen different types of the formula culminating in an attempt at a cargo-carrier which he named the Poucargo. At 800 kg, this could take five parachutists plus pilot. Of the various Croses types, more than 200 were built. First registered in August 1968 and built by Guy Flicot of Abbeville, F-PPPI was destroyed there on April 9th 1977.

From the Mignet formula came Emilien Croses' tandem-winged Criquet and from this Guy Flicot of Abbeville developed the Croses-Flicot CF-1 Mini-Criquet. Registered F-PVQI in August 1974, it flew between 1975 and licence expiry in 1977 after which it was given to the Musée de l'Air at Le Bourget where this picture was taken on June 6th 1981.

Originally built in 1957, this Croses EC-1 is the second of its type to have been built. The product of Emilien Croses of Macon, F-WIHL is a Mignet-formula aircraft. The addition of a trailing edge control surface on the rear wing – visible in this picture as a linear discontinuity, makes this an attractive, easy-to-fly two-seater. Fifty years on it was still flying.

In some ways, Croses' variations on the Mignet theme made for better-looking light aircraft. As much as anything else, the undercarriages were always robust in appearance while the main wing bracing and control was better engineered.

Now registered F-PIHL, the Croses EC-1 shows off its dramatic, eye-catching planform.

Constructed in 1962 by Raymond Gauthier and Gilbert Landray at Macon, F-PKMZ was a Croses EC-1 Goéland, the third to be built. Note the two trim tabs attached to the outer portions of the top or main wing. It was destroyed at Lachaise on June 15th 1988.

Emilien Croses, Henri Mignet's great friend and admirer, was based at Macon (Saone-et-Loire) and built his Pouplume as the smallest and lightest airframe then possible. Power was provided by a mostly-exposed 10 hp Monet Goyon motorcycle engine of 230cc. The empty weight was just 231 lbs and, with pilot and fuel, 441 lbs.

This close-up view of the Pouplume's nose shows the clever power installation. A separate propeller shaft was carried above the engine, the connection with the engine being by chain and sprocket providing a 3.5:1 reduction gear. This gave a propeller speed of a highly-efficient 1,300 rpm enabling a large-diameter airscrew to be used.

The prototype Croses Pouplume takes its place at the end of a line-up of various models of Mignet Flying Fleas – all, characteristically, of different sizes and with a wide variety of engines.

July, 1961, and Emilien Croses' EAC 103 Pouplume No.1, F-PKFA, attracts plenty of attention at its first public showing. The name translates as 'Flea Feathers'. Notice the relatively large and coarse-pitch propeller, an indication that it is slow turning.

As we have seen, the tandem-wing formula can be traced back almost to the pioneering days of flight. Indeed, the most memorable early example of this was the record 6-hour flight of Alexis Maneyrol in Louis Peyret's glider on October 21st 1922 at Itford and its subsequent performances in the Lympne Light Aeroplane Trials. The formula, later capitalised on by Henri Mignet, did not escape the attention of other designers. Peyret had progressed to the astonishing Taupin of 1937 (F-APAC) which put up an impressive series of pre-war records. Developed from the glider, this was powered by a 90 hp Régnier inverted inline engine. His work within the SFCA (Société Française de Construction Aéronautique) was continued by Jean G Louis Lignel who built his L.44 No.1 during 1944 while the war was still raging. Completed, it first flew as F-WAIC on December 21st 1946, later becoming F-PAIC. Powered by a Renault of 74 hp, Lignel named the L.44 Cross Country and in this picture, taken at its Toussous-le-Noble base on May 13th, 1952, the aircraft (now bearing the markings F-BAIC) has been grounded here for want of a battery. Unlike the Flying Flea, the Lignel's wings were well separated, the front (of greater span) fitted with ailerons than could also be used in tandem (in this view they are, strangely, both 'up') and the rear wing carrying a full-span elevator.

Opposite: Emilien Croses investigated the idea of making the Mignet formula into a 'commercial' proposition and in 1976 designed and built the biggest machine ever to appear based on the Flying Flea. The Croses B-EC 9 Paras Cargo was powered by a 180 hp Lycoming, had a five-wheeled undercarriage (four front, one rear) and was intended for light freight duties or for sky-jumpers. The capacious fuselage could hold five parachutists and the door was a convenient roller-blind type that spooled up into the roof like the door on the Vickers Vimy Commercial fifty years earlier. Only one example was ever built, initially registered F-PYBG and later, as pictured here, as F-AZVC. Croses died in November 2006 at the grand age of 90.

The manoeuvrability of the Lignel was later demonstrated at Toussous-le-Noble as the owner flew around with the door held open and an extended arm waving. Notice in this view how the fuselage flares to considerable width at the two-seater side-by-side pilot/passenger cabin.

Stability at very low speeds is one characteristic of this extraordinary development of the tailless tandem-wing or, to be correct, the super-staggered tailless biplane. In this design, as in Louis Peyret's 1922 tandem-wing glider, both wings are almost equal in span and chord. Additionally, both have trailing-edge control surfaces.

The unusual plan-form of the Lignel is seen to advantage in this low-level fly-by view.

While the designers who experimented with variations on Mignet's formula were legion, they also played an on going part in the evolution of designs. Emilian Croses' work was continued by Yves and Alain Croses while a stream of others contributed their sous-worth to the Pou. Jean de la Farge moved from France to Argentina where, in 1960, he built his La Pulga en Pacheco which was an HM-293-like machine but with a tailplane fixed above a fixed fin – the first 'T'-tailed Flea. In Italy the hybrid Lavorini Pou appeared in 1981, an aircraft with two wings of almost equal span. Lavorini's second design was a futuristic machine with wide-spread wheels and a pusher engine. Gilbert Landray's ultra-sleek Fleas combined with the efforts of masters such as Claude Piel and Françoise Lederlin. An extremely small and unmarked Flea variant is pictured at Popham in August 1995. Despite its diminutive proportions and what is clearly a tiny engine driving a three-blade plastic propeller, it flew extremely well.

Old-timers are said to complain that hand-starting an aeroplane with a three-blade propeller increases the chances of rapped knuckles by fifty percent. Be that as it may, this French Flea flyer happily twists the plastic airscrew on the sharp end of his tiny Flea variant on a visit to Popham Airfield in Hampshire in 1995.